D0953455

The Irony of Manifest Destiny

The Irony of Manifest Destiny

The Tragedy of America's Foreign Policy

WILLIAM PFAFF

WALKER & COMPANY
NEW YORK

Published by Walker Publishing Company, Inc., New York

All papers used by Walker & Company are natural, recyclable products
made from wood grown in well-managed forests. The manufacturing
processes conform to the environmental regulations of the country of origin.

LIBRARY OF CONGRESS CATALOGING-IN-PUBLICATION DATA
HAS BEEN APPLIED FOR.

ISBN: 978-0-8027-1699-6

Visit Walker & Company's Web site at www.walkerbooks.com

First U.S. edition 2010

1 3 5 7 9 10 8 6 4 2

Typeset by Westchester Book Group
Printed in the United States of America by Worldcolor Fairfield

To Juliet, Alexander, James, Josephine, and Jason,
To their mothers and their fathers,
Alexandra and Adamandia, Fréderic and Nicholas,
And to their wise and beautiful grandmother

The knowledge of past events is the sovereign corrective of human nature.
—Polybius of Megalopolis
(ca. 201–120 B.C.)

Show me a hero, and I'll write you a tragedy.
—F. Scott Fitzgerald,
"Notebooks," *The Crack-Up*

We will export death and violence to the four corners of the earth in defense of our great nation.
—George W. Bush (quoted in
Bob Woodward, *Bush at War*, 2003)

Things bad begun make strong themselves by ill . . .
For mine own good,
All causes shall give way: I am in blood
Stepp'd insofar, that should I wade no more, Returning were
as tedious as go o'er . . .
strange things I have in head, that will to hand,
which must be acted, ere they may be scanned.
. . . we are yet but young in deed.
—*Macbeth*, Act III

Contents

An Introductory Note

This essay proposes an interpretation of the transformation in Western Enlightenment civilization between the founding political events of modern times, the French Revolution and the creation of the American Republic, and our twentieth- and twenty-first-century experience of extreme ideological violence.

It is primarily addressed to Americans, as the United States is the most influential, as well as the most powerful contemporary nation and is committed to a secular utopian ideology of universal democracy: an intellectually unsustainable idea as well as politically impossible to achieve, hence a cause for global concern. As Kenneth Minogue, the Australian political philosopher, has observed, a political ideology is implicitly a project to control the world.[1]

This is inevitably a work of sweeping, "journalistic" generalizations, many of which may give the reader pause, as departing from the conventional opinion. However, both its argument and its general conclusions are founded in the realities of the present day. Religion has a larger place in my discussion than is usual in books of this kind. It is conspicuously absent from much serious political discussion, except when invoked as the cause of irrational violence or as an

idiosyncratic factor in American domestic politics. Little attention is paid to the complexity of religion's power over
how men and women see, and have conducted themselves,
historically. This is a lamentable lacuna in the discussion.

My thesis develops from the Western Enlightenment's
substitution of secular for religious assumptions about society, human values, and destiny: the subject of Chapter II.
This changed the expectations held in the West about human progress, and put secular utopian aspirations or expectations in place of those religious beliefs and hopes that
previously had dominated Western civilization and Western thought. It thereby deeply altered subsequent history. It
was responsible for the extreme violence of the twentieth
century and, it may prove, the twenty-first.

The era in which we live began with Allied victory in the
Second World War, the objective of the Allied coalition; but
the progressive administration of Franklin Delano Roosevelt
had a secondary goal, which was to put an end to European
imperialism, seen in Washington as an obstacle to a large
and generous reformation of the international system. The
Axis defeated, the Soviet-Western alliance disappointed these
ambitions by metamorphosizing into the Cold War between
the Soviet Union and the West that continued until 1989.
While the European empires collapsed, most of their former
colonies experienced much difficulty in establishing stable
sovereign governments.

International war, usually undeclared, proved not to be
over. It subsequently was waged by the United States and
various of its allies in Korea in 1950–1953, in Vietnam in
the 1960s–1970s, and in the last few years twice against the

Saddam Hussein government in Iraq, and then against the insurrectionary eruption caused by the second Iraq intervention, and against the Taliban government in Afghanistan, and subsequently against the Taliban insurrection. Informal international conflict, involving major states, continues today in the Middle East. The American military or quasi-military interventions in the Caribbean and Central America in the 1950s and after were continuation of a century-old semi-imperialism, exploitative if paternalistic, justified in the North American mind by the Monroe Doctrine. Concern about the possibility of future major wars is responsible for the present deployment of American forces in some one thousand U.S. military bases and stations throughout the world.[2]

This surely was not what President Roosevelt and the American people had in mind during the final months of the Second World War. Nor did they expect a Cold War with the Soviet Union, with the domination of Europe at issue, or with the Chinese Communists.

What has occurred since 1945 has amounted to an American effort to control the consequences of the twentieth-century crisis in Europe and the breakdown of imperial order in Asia, the Near and Middle East, and latterly in Africa, while maintaining that supervisory role over the Americas first claimed by the United States in 1823. All this has been done with the best of intentions, as in the ultimate interests of the beneficiaries of American attentions, as well as serving what have been conceived to be American national interests, combining to form a harmonious whole.

These are the subjects of my third and fourth chapters, and the fifth chapter is devoted to the character of what unfortunately has become an unnecessary and unwinnable war by the United States against radical currents in the Islamic religion.

This all occurs within a conception of "manifest" American destiny, initially articulated during the transcontinental expansion of the nineteenth century, matured in twentieth-century world affairs, now extended far beyond the continental limits within which it was first imagined.[3] My final chapter provides my conclusions, which regrettably are sober, even apprehensive.

I

A Manifest Destiny

THE ENLIGHTENMENT BROKE the continuity of Western history and civilization in many ways, but one aspect of what then happened seems little understood; yet it is of great importance today, as the United States makes a bid to consolidate its ideological assumptions and historical legacy in a universalization of the power and leadership it has assumed since the collapse of the Soviet Union.

Before the era of monotheistic religion in the Mediterranean world, religious controversy and speculation over the origin and nature of man and creation, and over the existence or nonexistence of an identifiable creator, arose from the philosophical reflections or rationales of individual cultures and societies. From these ultimately came Western monotheism, which has since been accepted as one of the defining characteristics of Western civilization. The Jewish prophets asserted that there was One God, revealed to them as "I Who Am," or, as Isaiah quoted God, "Apart from me, all is nothing." Christianity, of Judaic origin, was considered by Christians to be an elaboration of the messianic fulfillment of the One God's intentions with respect to mankind. Islam, subsequently, was in its own view a further extension of existing divine prophecies, and foresaw the completion of God's plan.

The Enlightenment substituted a secular utopianism for the religious beliefs about a celestial future that had been all but universal in Western society since antiquity. The Enlightenment proposed that there was no God (or if there should be one, he occupied a distant position as primordial "clockmaker" to existence, far from human concerns). What Peter Gay, the American historian of the Enlightenment, calls the Modern Paganism was substituted.[1]

This much is uncontroversial. One consequence of this, however, seems not to have been fully understood, or to have been widely ignored or denied. This is the connection of Enlightenment secularism to the terrible turn taken by Western history in the nineteenth and twentieth centuries. The ideological extremism that emerged in the nineteenth and early twentieth centuries, and what may be called the exterminatory violence of the 1914–1918 war, followed by the "totalitarian" ideological movements that characterized the twentieth century, are related to the secularization of Western utopian thought.

A powerful universalizing utopian ambition exists in Western civilization, a creativity and desire for power that have given the West overall global domination since the Renaissance. I do not say this in particular celebration of the West, but to state a reality. The West's history is distinguished by a creativity and dynamism that have allowed it to shape the modern world, and also by much violence and ruthless aggrandizement as well. The West is what it is, and we are its products.

The classical and religious cultures that formed the West assumed their ideas to be of universal validity. There was a Greek cultural adventurism and moral daring expressed in the myths of Prometheus, who seized fire from the gods for the benefit of mankind, and of Pandora, the first woman, sent by Zeus to punish humans and their Promethean benefactor by way of an incorrigible curiosity that caused her to open the box containing all of the ills that would ever after afflict mankind. She also appears among us as the Jews' and Christians' Eve. She is essential to our humanity.

In the centuries of Western religious belief that preceded the Enlightenment, utopian expectations were essentially religious and their fulfillment lay outside the limits of human life and time. Perfection and true happiness could only be found in the afterlife. The New Paganism of the European Enlightenment in the late seventeenth century, and the French Revolution that followed a century later, changed the fundamental nature of the envisaged utopia from religious redemption to secular transformation.

Now utopia had to be fulfilled within human time, and on earth. This made utopian thinking extremely dangerous, above all in a modern Western society that has largely repudiated the idea of "eternal" values and norms, and makes its own rules of conduct, sometimes high-minded and altruistic, and sometimes not. If God is dead, as the Enlightenment asserted, nothing is prohibited—as Dostoyevsky concluded—other than what we decide to prohibit to ourselves.

Every modern effort to universalize a nation's power and values so as to establish a "new" human society has rested upon Western illusions of progress that were understood by the Attic Greeks to be illusions, preoccupying Greek myth, religion, and philosophy. This survives in a variety of philosophic and artistic formulations, including the Greek tragedies themselves. The same understanding appears in the medieval Christian conception of Faust and the temptation to seize total power or knowledge through the agency of Satan, at the cost of one's eternal soul.

The common theme is that human effort to attain preeminence and unlimited power or knowledge carries a cost; it "presumes" on God or the gods, and is punished by them— or by "fate." Power produces hubris, defiance of the gods or of the appropriate human order, and this is punished. Tragedy accompanies the exercise of power; and pride ends in ruin. Tragedy follows guilt, according to Aristotle: unavoidable guilt on the part of a person of high spiritual or moral status.

As a general proposition applied to international relations this has a very old human warrant and might be called the Greek Paradigm or Paradox since it is known today mostly by way of the classical Greek theater and specifically from Greek tragedy. Hubris causes overreaching, which meets defeat and retribution. Modern societies are not exempt.

SECULAR UTOPIANISM EXISTS in two versions. One is idealistic political action to obtain an unlikely or difficult but attainable goal. After 1945 many worked successfully for a united and peaceful Western Europe, however utopian such a goal seemed amid the ruins of the Second World War. In the 1950s many Americans thought it utopian to expect racial integration, and all but inconceivable that there could be a black American president. Others would have considered it hopelessly utopian to think that without a war the Soviet Union would ever give up its ideology, and of its own accord come to peaceful terms with the Western countries.

By contrast, the utopianism of a millenarian or transformational kind promises the emergence of a New Man, a "great dawn" providing an ultimate resolution of the human story that makes sense of everything that has gone before. This is a secular substitution for religious belief. Anarchism was such a doctrine in the late nineteenth and early twentieth centuries. It proposed by acts of terrorism to undermine or discredit existing systems of government and society, revealing their oppressive nature and inspiring people to rise up against them. The rejection of existing society was expected to liberate man's "natural" disposition to peaceful cooperation. This romantic notion reflected the Enlightenment idea that civilization corrupts the original innocence and reasonableness of humans.

Something like this was believed by many young people during the upheavals of 1968 and after in Europe and the United States, and later during the period of a certain European and North American enthusiasm for "Maoism" that resulted in "Red Brigade" bombings, murders, and kidnappings, all in the cause of permanent human happiness. Certain sectarian Trotskyite parties still exist that profess the transformation of human society through a "permanent revolution," whatever that may be.

THE RISE OF modern violence, as in the events of the French Revolution, accompanied the Enlightenment quest for a secular utopia. The French revolutionary wars were meant to defend the Revolution itself against foreign intervention, and to universalize popular republican government by the overthrow of hereditary rule throughout Europe. Napoleon, whom Hegel at first celebrated as embodying the "world spirit" of the Enlightenment age, began by defying the prevailing military codes and rules of eighteenth-century limited warfare, which is one reason for his initial successes. He subsequently made profound reforms in European political and social institutions. Their success caused him to appropriate them as the foundation for his own Empire, appointing his generals and his relations as princes of his realm. Though his career ended in military defeat at Waterloo, most of his reforms endured, which is not true of the secular revolutionaries who have followed him. Nonetheless, with his career, an exemplary historical pattern was evident, that of the Greek Paradigm, when prideful ambition inspires overreaching and defiance of the gods, ending in ruinous defeat: Heroic ambition, Hubris, Nemesis.

Beginning with the French Revolution and Napoleon, there have been a series of efforts by ideological leaders in individual nations to establish European—and, in the twentieth century, international—political and military domination in the name of a secular utopian theory, representing

the ideas of a group newly come to power, or the new artic-
ulation or rationalization of forces already at work in a society. The new ideology typically is put forward as the next
and concluding step in human liberation.

In each case, the nation concerned holds that its advanced
system of values and political vision has outmoded the prevailing international and national systems, requiring them
to be destroyed and replaced, necessitating, as well, the repudiation of established legal and moral norms of society
and of the international community, so as to make it possible to install its new world order.

This was the case with the George W. Bush administration,
even leaving aside the issues of human rights, torture, and
wars of aggression. From early in the war in Iraq, Condoleezza
Rice called for discarding the Westphalian international system of autonomous and sovereign nations, a system which implied the need for a diplomacy of balance of power, achieved
through negotiation and alliance. She (implicitly) advocated
its replacement by American global leadership.[2] Historically,
in each new attempt to overturn the international order and
replace it with a new ideological system, or with the hegemony
of one superior nation, the effort has proven unreasonable,
provoking wide and ultimately successful resistance. The goal
has proven impossible to achieve.*

---

* The Westphalian peace settlement of 1648 ended the Thirty Years'
  War and effectively marked the end of the Holy Roman Empire. It replaced it with the system of individual states possessing (theoretically)
  absolute sovereignty that continues to the present day, notwithstanding the existence of such international organizations as the United
  Nations or the European Union, to which members have voluntarily,
  but not irrevocably, ceded some degree of their national sovereignty.

The record of these efforts writes the history of the twentieth century. To begin with the most dramatic case, Adolf
Hitler arrogated to himself a project for European unification and eventual Nordic or "Aryan" world leadership, accompanied by "purification" and reordering of the human
race through eugenic measures that included the destruction of human groups deemed "unfit" to exist.*

Stalin, a successful provincial revolutionary, was led by the
theory of a dialectical and predetermined historical process,
taken from Marx and Lenin, to employ state power to assist
history to its necessary conclusion in rule by the working
class (which was to say, by its self-appointed "vanguard," the
leaders of the Bolshevik Party). It was an undertaking inherently incredible, but became believed in by millions, until
undone by its cruelty and futility. By contrast, Fidel Castro's
Cuban revolution, and the Marxist revolutionaries in Southeast Asia in the 1950s and 1960s, found in Marxism a popular
dynamism applicable to nationalist objectives—which are
not utopian in the transformational sense.†

---

* Eugenics was a theory influential at the time in many ostensibly progressive societies, including Britain, Scandinavia, and the United
States; it was a form of Darwinism intended to improve humanity.

† The pattern I describe does not extend to Japan's effort in the 1930s
and 1940s to create a Greater East Asian Coprosperity Sphere, as Japan
at the time was a nationalist and racist state, but not an ideological one,
meaning that its model of society was not exportable, and its motives
were purely imperial and strategic. Maoism, later, was a utopian ideological system exploiting Chinese nationalist sentiments, but (charac-
teristically for China) was never intended for export, even though it
acquired many Western admirers who themselves attempted to import

cont'd.

The admixture of fantasy and romanticism in Nazism and Bolshevism was fatal to them.[3] They would have failed even if they had not been defeated in war. Theirs were "unnatural" expectations—as Mikhail Gorbachev and his associates ultimately understood, when they finally acknowledged the Soviet system's failure and launched glasnost—"truth-telling."

Fascism in Italy, where it began, was on the other hand a version of romantic nationalism whose objective was the creation of a new Roman Empire, impossible militarily and politically for twentieth-century Italy, but not unimaginable. While it attracted nationalist (and anti-Semitic—which Italian Fascism initially was not) imitators in Romania, Hungary, and elsewhere, it was never an international movement as such, nor a transcendant and transformational ideology. When Mussolini died, so did Fascism, other than for a few Italian nostalgics. Nazism, because of its base in the notion of a superior "race," has a marginal international survival, including in the United States.

We are astounded today to think that at the time educated people actually believed Nazi racial theories, or Communism's naive notion of an eventual proletarian paradise. But millions did. The Khmer Rouge in Cambodia, like the Chinese Communists in their "Great Leap Forward"

---

† *cont'd.*

its ideas, always with disastrous consequences. A contrast is provided by the modern Islamist extremist groups that employ terrorism. Although the binding ideology is religious, the actual goals are a political utopia from which corrupting Western forces and values have been expelled to make possible the avowed (and unattainable) goal of global conversion to Islam and universal acceptance of Shari'a law.

and "Cultural Revolution," justified humiliation and murder of the bourgeoisie, intellectuals, and even the merely
educated and those corrupted by living in cities, so as to
give humanity a new start and a renewed innocence.

In each of these cases, the effort to achieve the new program so as to change man and society has caused or provoked
a destructive war or campaign of oppression. Violence in the
service of a secular utopia has consistently tended to be re-
morseless and total—since so much is at stake, with so little
time to achieve it. "What vileness would you not commit . . .
to change the world?" the German Communist poet Bertolt
Brecht asked in 1931. The answer was found in the practices
of the Soviet and Nazi states.

THE UNITED STATES, with its traditions of pragmatism and
practicality, and the national myth of unlimited opportunity,
has not in the past been susceptible to this kind of ideology.
Its style has been populist and nationalist. Since abandoning
isolationism, however, and in search of an international vo-
cation, the nation's ideological immunity has waned, and the
utopianism of the nation's origins recurs. The American conception of Manifest Destiny, originally seen as transcontinental expansion, has been recast since the time of Woodrow
Wilson as the creation of a world order that is nominally plu-
ralistic but under ultimate American leadership—which, it is
taken for granted, would be welcome to nearly all.

A program to bring the world to democracy reflects a
large consensus of views in the American professional foreign and political communities today. It constitutes a ver-

sion of secular utopian thought that sees man as "naturally" democratic if only he can be freed from the repressive national, cultural, and religious bonds that confine him, and if the despots who rule him are removed. It is a highly romantic view of society that demonstrates how far the policy's main modern theoreticians, most of whom in the George W. Bush administration identified themselves as neoconservatives, have actually been from real conservatism, and how close to a sentimental leftism.*

Their view of how this transformation of international society is to come about, which has roots deep in the American political consciousness and history (including the liberal and Democratic party traditions), envisages the democracies initially forming an association or federation under American leadership (or in another and highly unlikely version, the transformation of a much-strengthened NATO into a political as well as security federation). In whatever version, it reflects the policy tradition that in the past produced the League of Nations and the United Nations, both great disappointments to Washington because they included no effective executive power. The group now envisaged would form a political union that would also have a common economy. (The international credit collapse that began in America in 2008 cooled enthusiasm for a deregulated capitalist economic and trading system centered upon the United States.)

A federation of the democracies is powerfully seductive to American policy elites. It was in the presidential platform

---

* Conservatism: "Disposed to maintain existing institutions or views; opposed to change; adhering to sound principles . . ." *Webster's New International Dictionary*, Second Edition.

of John McCain in 2008 and was endorsed as a goal by Barack Obama. It is fair to say that among American political and professional foreign policy elites, including those prominent in the Obama administration, this, or something very much like it, is widely (if vaguely) assumed to be the ultimate objective of American foreign policy. It is unrealistic, and has virtually no chance of occurring.[4]

PREVIOUSLY, WHEN RELIGION dominated nations and the moral reasoning and expectations of the societies of Western civilization, the meaning of human existence, its necessary norms, and the future of mankind were usually understood in the terms provided by religious prophecy and doctrine. It was a human duty to analyze, understand, and respect these doctrines. To set one's own interpretation of the universe against that believed to have been revealed by God and his prophets was presumption, heresy, or indeed madness.

The secular era has no divine reference, and frequently has constructed its substitute for that reference in the form of a synthetic religion whose god is the nation and people themselves. For that reason the modern political ideology has generally proven to be a project to control the world. The nature of an ideology is the purported discovery of the universal truth about society and history, implying a line of action necessary to conform to or exploit this discovery. A program is implied, and a national policy.

The United States has dramatically departed from the isolation of its colonial origins into the global arena to become the ideologically expansionist military power it is today. Why and how this happened is important to understand, along with the historical and cultural circumstances that shaped this development. For the United States, this is comprehensible only in the context of the Western rationalist civilization that has existed since the time of the Enlightenment. American ideology now claims to know the direction in which history is headed. It proposes an explanation of the role being played—or that should be played—by the American state, as well as suggesting the risks of that role. This is presented in the language of pragmatism, as well as of national interest, international interest, and world peace. But it amounts to a nationalist American ideology.

The implications of this are dangerous to the United States, to its allies, and to international peace, because of its lack of realism. The American project to bring democracy to a recalcitrant world has already, under the Clinton and two Bush administrations, produced in the first decade of the new century a series of unsuccessful military interventions in weaker societies, with a fragile truce (at this writing) in Iraq, a second war in Afghanistan that risks a destructive American military and political intervention in nuclear-armed Pakistan, and failed or inconclusive interventions in Somalia and other parts of Africa and Arabia.

The current enemy, identified as "Islamic terrorism," consists of an ensemble of groups making up a number of separate if related movements of nationalist, puritanical, and anti-Western political reform, of religious inspiration, active in several parts of the Muslim world. Such a movement is implanted in a part of the ethnic and linguistic community composed of the forty million Pashtuns of Pakistan, Afghanistan, and Central Asia, unconquered since the time of Alexander the Great.

A CERTAIN TRADITION of political realism in the interpretation of international affairs, influential in the American government during the period between the last world war and the fall of the Soviet Union, now has been abandoned. Associated with George F. Kennan, author of the Containment policy; with another distinguished diplomat, Charles Bohlen; and with the theologian Reinhold Niebuhr and certain other major twentieth-century American diplomatic and intellectual figures, it was responsible for the analysis that identified the postwar Soviet Union as a dangerous and expansionist ideological power whose ambitions needed to be calmly appraised, "contained," and countered by American policy and that of the other wartime Allies.[5] This went against much sentimentality among Americans during the last year of the Second World War and the early postwar years about the legacy of the Popular Front, gratitude for the immense Russian war effort, and a popular notion of Stalin as a benevolent figure (whom Roosevelt told Churchill he was confident he "could handle").

"Containment," despite its militarization during the 1950s, was ultimately a great success, due to the reality perceived in 1951 by Kennan that the Soviet "grand design [was] a futile and unachievable one, persistence in which promises no solution of their own predicaments and dilemmas," so that its containment offered the prospect of "eventual breakup or gradual mellowing of Soviet power," which in fact occurred, exactly as predicted.

In place of this modest, humane, and effective realism about the Soviet Union, the United States in the late twentieth and early twenty-first centuries has substituted a political ideology based on faith in universal human progress toward democracy, validating the superiority of American institutions, ideas, and practices. During the Clinton and George W. Bush administrations, this faith hardened in the face of the terrorist challenge, and was recast as authorizing aggressive international intervention, and when necessary military preemption, to destroy obstacles to the American vision of the future—a policy that George W. Bush said in his second inaugural address amounted to an American mission to abolish evil from the world (a task in the past ordinarily thought reserved to God).

Eventually the conception of America's enemy became extended to radicalism of most kinds, to disorderly states, conflict, and failure in the non-Western world, to poverty and social disorder ("breeding grounds" for terrorism—as President Obama reiterated in March 2009, when justifying interventions into Pakistan), as well as to "rogue nations," meaning those that defy the United States. A senior figure in the Washington policy community, listing what were "increasingly agreed" (in summer 2008) to be the "nontraditional" threats to Europe and America, began with "terrorist groups of global reach and potential access to weapons of mass destruction," and continued with "WMD diversification and proliferation, failed states, organized crime, access to energy, climate change, pandemics, and more." He urged a "complex mixture of military and civilian capabilities along with a combination of institutional tools, both national and multilateral," to resolve them.[6]

This left out resurgent superpowers (presumably "traditional" threats), but otherwise would seem to add up to war against most of international society's failings in the early twenty-first century. One might think the challenge uninviting to even the most utopian, optimistic, and ambitious of American leaders.

II

The Enlightenment Invention of Secular Utopia

T HE ENLIGHTENMENT IS TODAY understood as the intellectual movement that liberated the Western mind from
religious authority—or, as it was said, from religious superstition and ignorance. It proclaimed God's death, or at least
his displacement to a remote and impersonal role in the
universe. It made men mortal, denying that salvation could
be expected in an afterlife. Therefore a perfected world had
to be made in the here and now. This was taken to require,
or license, unprecedented measures to make people free and
happy. It produced an immense psychological change as well
as transforming the life of the mind—of thought itself, which
now had to be taken as solipsistic and transient, and not as
part of an established and eternal dialogue. The Enlightenment also inadvertently changed the nature of war, removing
the limits imposed by Christian belief in human immortality
and divine judgment. War was now logically limited only by
reason and utility.

Enlightenment thought examined theology to find ways to reconcile it with the new secular currents inspired by the philosophy and humanist values of classical Greece, redis-covered in Europe at the time of the Renaissance, thanks to the preservation of classical texts by Arab scholars.[1] Europe-ans found themselves expected to live without an accepted structure of spiritual recourse or guidance; with only the resources of individual reason or unreasoned choice; with-out norms that transcended individual existence. Thus the ambition of the writers of the American Declaration of Independence—mostly Deists*—was no more than to en-able the "pursuit" of happiness. Their theologian predeces-sors had proposed how to guarantee perpetual happiness. The religious "utopianism" of Christianity concerned the afterlife, because that was where "utopia"—eternal life—existed, at least in Christian belief. Enlightened thinkers had to act within the confines of time.

The European Enlightenment assumed the possibility of a secular solution to human history. It asserted the ability of men and women to create a perfected society on earth. The Enlightenment led to the revolutions that ended the politi-cal and social domination of Western society by religion and an hereditary aristocracy.

THE IMAGE OF a New World provided by the discovery and exploration of the Americas, whether conceived as a lost

---

* Believers in a God-creator remote from the realm of human experience.

paradise, or reinforcing hope that reason and science had now empowered men to reform humanity, inspired a belief in eventual perfection of human society that remains widely accepted today. The argument for original innocence is incredible, disproved by history itself, as is the proposition of a utopian future, discredited by the events of the twentieth century and by what we have so far seen of the twenty-first, as well as by history. But most Americans and Europeans continue to assume that the solutions for mankind lie ahead of us, and that the failures of the past were caused by trust in myth rather than in reason. This is an assertion of the moral responsibility of mankind, but expresses a claim which, like religion, rests on faith rather than material evidence.

The European intellectual world in the sixteenth and seventeenth centuries was greatly influenced by the findings of the maritime explorers, proving the existence of important and sophisticated non-Christian civilizations and cultures, and challenging the Christian claim to exclusive truth about God and his relation to human society: thus introducing relativist perceptions and skepticism concerning conventional thought and existing institutions. In the sixteenth century, Montaigne's persistent question in his essays had already been "what do I know?" (*ques'que j'sois?*), a critical reexamination of the culture and morality of Christian Europe and its theological presuppositions.

Enlightenment thinkers attempted to reconstruct philosophy and morality from a position of radical doubt (believed to be essential to a scientific approach to reality).

Thus Descartes's system begins with his affirmation of existence: "I think, therefore I exist." If he could know without doubt that he existed, he could explore what logically followed, and although his conclusions were subsequently contested, his thought and his system of thinking survived as one of the foundations of the Enlightenment consciousness, and they remain today a force in French intellectual life.

The assumed validity of Enlightenment principles logically implied their universalization. If truth was universally valid, knowledge should be made universally known. Science should replace Biblical accounts of human existence. Darwin in the nineteenth century was to produce one such account, which he meant to be of purely scientific reference, that of natural selection in the development of animal and botanical life, but the unvoiced implication was that the same was true for man, and the unsettling conclusion was that natural selection would go on.

The Enlightenment repudiation of religion opened the quest for a secular utopia, a new resolution of the Western drive to progress that could reconcile human divisions and reveal the supposed ultimate harmonies of the human experience. European elites had since the Renaissance speculated about utopias in such works as Francis Bacon's *The New Atlantis* (1627). It was thought then (and again in the Enlightenment generation) that an ideal society had existed in the distant past (a Golden Age; the classical Greeks had themselves written about the existence of Atlantis). The society of the earlier age had supposedly been corrupted by civilization. Thus Rousseau and others (including many of our twenty-first-century contemporaries) believed in the innate goodness of people that would reemerge in an ideal society, once corruption and tyranny could be swept away.*

The Enlightenment assumption that religious superstition had been chiefly responsible for past violence and war, something widely taken for granted today in the new religious controversies of the twenty-first century, has to be considered with an understanding of the missionary assumptions of Christianity from its beginning, and subsequently those of Islam, producing the Crusades, and eventually of the Reformed Churches, culminating in the terrible wars of religion eventually ended at Westphalia in 1648.

CHRISTIANITY WAS A missionary religion because it considered itself commissioned to convey God's message to the "Gentiles," meaning all the non-Jewish world. This mission to convert the world rapidly became a political affair which the Roman authorities attempted to suppress: a new and classless religion that enjoined Christians to obey the state, accept military service, and pay taxes, but simultaneously

---

* The American neoconservative idea in 2003 that a "new Middle East" would emerge once Saddam Hussein and other despots were overthrown was a sad corruption of this distant idea, but so are many modern ideas. Corporate America and Republican politicians for many years preceding 2008's global capitalist economy crisis held that "big government" is the modern problem, and that the unfettered market would prove to be an expression of innate human reason and justice. Their belief in the collectively infallible rationality of the market echoed the utopian Socialists, such as Charles Fourier, Pierre-Joseph Proudhon, and Robert Owen, visionary Socialist predecessors of such utopian capitalists as Alan Greenspan (and his mentor, Ayn Rand).

claimed the allegiance of all Christians in matters that were not "Caesar's" but "God's"—a God replacing the Roman gods and therefore a subversive force.

The Jews have never fought a war in order to spread their religion (although since the founding of the modern state of Israel they have certainly defended their country and sought to extend the territories they control). The Christians and Muslims have always done so: in the Crusades, in the Christian conquest of Eastern Europe, the Baltic states, and Russia in order to deliver the Christian Scripture, in the conquest and exploration of the Americas and Asia to convert their "pagan" populations, and so on into Africa, the Pacific Islands, the Far North. The Arabs' explosions out of Arabia in the eighth and ninth centuries to conquer all the Eastern Mediterranean, the North African coast to the Atlantic, Spain, France as far as Poitiers, and through the Balkans to Vienna were military conquests inspired by their new religion, although the evolution into political empire began early.

The Christian era had (and has) seen much violence in the course of struggles over doctrinal differences in order to suppress heresy, so as to prevent "error" from being propagated (logically, the purpose being to save even the enemies' souls, in jeopardy because of heresy). The Crusades were meant to free the Holy Land from the Muslim infidels, who were viewed as unfit to possess them and as oppressors of Christians, and the Muslims fought the Crusaders for the equivalent reasons. By the time of the Enlightenment, the Reformation and Counter-Reformation had already undermined European Christian belief in a single uncontestable religious truth. The Reformation's challenge to the Roman church rapidly acquired political form, reinforcing or rationalizing existing dynastic and political contests, or inspiring new ones as societies divided on lines of religious persuasion.

With Calvinism, the issue of theocracy reappeared, that of uncontested government by a single undisputable religious authority (as aspired to by Islamic integrists today, as in Iran). Calvinism attacked the separation of religious from secular or imperial authority that had generally prevailed as the fundamental assumption of the Holy Roman Empire. The Bishop of Rome had in the year 800 crowned Charlemagne as Emperor, signifying that pope and emperor each possessed legitimate authority in their separate realms, on the scriptural authority of Jesus of Nazareth that the things belonging to Caesar were to be rendered to Caesar, and things that belonged to God were owed to God.

Calvin's doctrine of predestination made its way from Geneva to John Knox's Scotland, to English and Dutch Puritanism, and eventually to the American New England colonies, where the sectarian millenarianism and unaccommodating religious beliefs of America's Puritan Pilgrim ancestors provided the United States with its founding myth, that of the City on the Hill, given a triumphalist appropriation for another age by Ronald Reagan.* The amalgamation

---

* The actual words of the first governor of the Massachusetts Bay Colony, John Winthrop, were: "For we must consider that we shall be as a city upon a hill, the eyes of all people are upon us; so that if we should deal falsely with our God in the work we have undertaken, and so cause Him to withdraw His present help from us, we shall shame the faces of many of God's worthy servants, and cause their prayers to be turned into curses." Aboard the ship *Arabella*, 1630.

of American Calvinism into what became mainstream American Protestantism (or its abandonment under the pressure of Enlightenment ideas) was an important contribution to American religious exceptionalism.

WARS AMONG CHRISTIANS concerning the control of populations, territories, and dynastic interests were inspired by the political motives that provide the common substance of history. They took place, however, within an intellectual and moral framework concerned with the exactitude of what Christians considered a revelation of divine truth and motivation yet to be delivered to the mass of mankind, that of Jesus of Nazareth.

His crucifixion and resurrection, in the New Testament account, revealed him as the Christ or Messiah foreseen in Jewish scriptures. His message was no longer directed only to God's chosen people, the Jews, who included all the original followers of Jesus. It was now a radically new mission, to convert the whole world to the belief of the Christians that there had been a divine intervention in history which the Apostles had witnessed, that of God's Son become man, and to foster belief in the mission among men of that third "person" of God described as the Holy Spirit (Holy Ghost, in his/her archaic but more pleasing appellation).

These claims themselves produced conflict among the Christians over the interpretation of doctrine, and also disagreements between territorial and political communities of Christians in the Roman empire, leading eventually, after Constantine the Great, to the doctrinal conflict between the bishops of the Eastern Roman Empire and those of the West, and to disputes over papal primacy among the bishops, an eminently political issue. These eventually caused the East-West schism in 1054, confirmed in 1472, that still exists.[2]

The wars pitting Christian believers against other Christians ordinarily were linked to the ambitions of bishops, princes, and dynasties, or to exercises of secular power by religious authorities. Conventional and chivalric moral limits were overridden in the Crusades, driven by the religious imperative to free the Holy Land from domination by Muslim unbelievers but often degenerating into politics and plunder (Innocent III said of the Fourth Crusade, in which the Venetian armies in 1204 sacked Christian Constantinople, the second city of the Christian Roman empire: "the Latins giving an example only of perversity and works of darkness"). By the time of the Great Schism, the Greeks, who had suffered quite enough collateral damage from the activities of the Western Crusader armies, said "better the sultan's turban than the pope's tiara."

THE PITILESS ALBIGENSIAN Crusade that took place within Europe in the thirteenth century succeeded in destroying the heretical Catharist movement in France. This was an ideological war, as were the other Crusades, but all had the peculiar and paradoxical character that they were meant to save even their enemies from the damnation that heresy or paganism implied. This is more or less what the Crusaders of the tenth to fourteenth centuries were offering Muslims: Become Christians; give up your false beliefs and accept ours, and we'll end the war.*

The Cathars were powerful in southern France, although the belief existed elsewhere in Western Europe; it had arrived from the Balkans, as the Cathar "Bogomils" living in what today is Muslim Bosnia migrated westward under Orthodox Christian pressure. The heresy itself had ancient sources, in Manichean and Gnostic thought. Cathars believed in a dualistic universe in which the New Testament God, ruler of spiritual things, warred against Satan, who ruled matter. (The Cathars who remained in their Balkan homes are thought to have converted to Islam as a means of resistance to their Christian enemies, and to compose the population now known as Bosniaks).

The Inquisition and Christian crusaders attacked the Cathars in France, brutally suppressing the movement, notably in a great massacre at Béziers in 1209, where no one was spared. Arnaud-Amalric, abbot of Cîteaux, made himself immortally infamous by saying, when asked how the heretics could be distinguished from the faithful in Béziers, "Burn them all. God will know his own!" This actually was, in principle, a sound statement of what he presumably believed. The crucial significance of intention in religious warfare is commonly ignored; in principle, its purpose is to

---

* One heard an echo of this in the radio appeal made by Osama bin Laden to the American people in 2007, proposing a simple way to end the wars in Iraq and Afghanistan: The Americans should give up Christianity and accept Islam.

destroy or limit the influence of heresy or religious error, so as to preserve the truth essential to humanity's salvation, and if possible to convert the unbeliever or heretic.

THE CLAIM THAT crusader war is mindless fanaticism, as made by John Gray in his otherwise brilliant book *Black Mass*, misses the point, as do the comparisons often made between crusader war and modern secular ideological war, such as the Second World War. Totalitarian war is intended to produce a permanent transformation in the nature of human society, the defining purpose of post-Enlightenment secular utopianism. The purpose of war against heretics was in the past conceived as saving them and others from the supposed deceits of Satan.

The purpose of twentieth-century war against kulaks, or the capitalist bourgeoisie, or what Comintern propagandists chose to describe as running dogs of imperialism, was to exterminate social classes that resist human progress, or in the Nazi case to destroy human groups such as the Jews as inferior beings unfit to live. It is the designated group's nature itself that makes the group an obstacle to the achievement of a new order. The heretic, on the other hand, can be converted to the truth. This is a capital point in understanding the difference between religious millenarianism and secular utopianism. Gray, for example, writes that the stated belief of George W. Bush that his government's "responsibility to history is clear: to . . . rid the world of evil," ultimately derives from a "Christian post-millenarianism, which harks back to the belief of the first Christians that the blemishes of human life can be wiped away in a benign catastrophe."[3] President Bush actually was giving voice to the ancient Manichean heresy that has become unwittingly assimilated into the apocalyptic fictions (themselves heretical, in terms of orthodox Protestant belief) of a sect of the American so-called "religious right," by whom the former American president seems to have been greatly (and disastrously) influenced.

The American invasion of Iraq and the Israeli displacement and repression of Palestinians also are seen by many theologically naive American fundamentalist Protestants as fulfilling apocalyptic prophesies in the Jewish and Christian scriptures. They are interpreted as preliminary to the prophesied "End Days" of earthly existence, which will bring the separation of the Saved—themselves and a limited number of other Christians belonging to specified denominations or sects, who have experienced a Pentecostal experience and "found Jesus"—who will be "raptured away" to heaven, while the rest of us, denominationally excluded Christians, all Muslims, and all those Jews unlucky enough not to have converted to Christian belief in the last instants before Armageddon's arrival, will go to hell. It's all in the Bible, they claim.

In this particular Protestant conception of mortal destiny, Muslims, Jews, and errant Christians are treated as lacking in personal responsibility for what happens to them; they are the assigned agents in a drama in which a limited number of Christians are predestined to salvation not by their virtue, since most of these believers are part of an ultimately Calvinist doctrinal tradition holding all of fallen man to be totally corrupt, but by the arbitrary choice of God. Predestinarianism has, of course, been a tormenting and controversial issue in Protestant theology since even before Calvin's time.

Apocalyptic sectarianism of this kind, together with other
utopian religious movements, have been fairly common in
Christian (and other) religious history, although more often
than not quietist, unworldly, and pacifist, as with the Mennonites and Amish (of Swiss Anabaptist descent), Quakers,
and Shakers. More dramatic theocratic utopias were established by the Calvinists in Geneva; by the Mormons' founder, Joseph Smith, in "burnt-over" upstate New York; and
by their counterparts elsewhere, including, of course, in the
Massachusetts Bay Colony, where they are celebrated as
America's Pilgrim fathers.

If we exclude the theologically eccentric contemporary
sects of American Christian apocalyptics, eager to be snatched
to heaven before the battle of Armageddon destroys everyone else, leaving existence unblemished, Christian eschatology generally has not expected John Gray's benign
catastrophe but a divine intervention to vindicate the elect
against their oppressors, raise the dead, judge mankind, and
establish a new creation. Such apocalyptic forecasts were frequent in the two or three centuries before and after the birth
of Jesus. "The" Apocalypse is the subject of the last book of
the New Testament, the book of Saint John. In it, John falls
into a trance and the bearer of prophecy identifies himself
by saying, "I am before all, I am at the end of all, and I live. I
who underwent death am alive, as you seest, to endless ages,
and I hold the keys of death and hell." While this is unmistakably a description of the Christians' Christ, the meaning

of the prophecy that follows is obscure and has always been treated with great circumspection by theologians.

DURING AND AFTER the Reformation both Catholic and Protestant authorities, while struggling against one another, also tried to contain or destroy such heretical or apocalyptic sects as the revolutionary Anabaptists, regarded as not only false but erratic, uncontrollable, and irrational. Rationalism and rational argument were dominant in mainstream Western Christianity, even if the fundamental Christian claim that God exists and has implicated Himself in human history seems to modern secular society inherently unreasonable. The established religious as well as political authorities naturally had heavy investments in order and orthodoxy.

Anglo-American intellectual and political circles during the late 1950s and after were greatly influenced by a wonderful book on the millenarian currents and sects of medieval and Reformation Europe, seeking earthly utopias. The author was the British scholar Norman Cohn, and the book was called *The Pursuit of the Millennium*.

His topic was suggested to him by his experiences as a military intelligence officer during the Second World War and his book was published at the height of the Cold War. It describes revolutionary, chiliastic (millenarian) movements such as the Flagellants and revolutionary Anabaptists among "the surplus population living on the margin" in medieval and Reformation Europe, whose leaders made "boundless, millennial" promises that inspired upheavals of great violence, meant to bring about the "utopia" of Christ's imminent return to rule the earth. Writing at the time he did, Cohn saw a connection between these prophets and their followers, and the leaders and followers of the Communist and Fascist totalitarian movements of the twentieth century. This seemed particularly true in the Fascist case because of certain parallels to the history of the revolutionary Anabaptists, who eventually ended in a cult of an amoral superman.

Cohn describes the pitiless suppression by church and civil authorities of the Anabaptists in Münster in 1535, where the Anabaptists had established an absolutist religious dictatorship and proclaimed a new revelation, their leader ordering and enforcing polygamy, terrorizing dissidents, and naming himself Monarch and Messiah of the Last Days. The struggle in which this ended pitted the illuminati-led utopian revolutionaries against the forces of political order and religious orthodoxy, outraged by the turbulence provoked by this fanatical, heretical, and subversive movement.[4]

THE CONSTRAINTS OF customary morality were tested to the limit in the sixteenth- and seventeenth-century wars of religion. Yet even the terrible Thirty Years' War, the great post-Reformation and Counter-Reformation struggle between Protestants and Catholics, was mainly a competition for secular power between Protestant and Catholic monarchs and princes. Both sides formally wanted the religious abdication of the other side. In fact, what practical people on both sides probably most wanted was restoration of the comfortable and singularly noncommittal and nondoctrinal (indeed, formally heretical) agreement of "cuius regio eius religio" that had prevailed before, meaning that people were expected to accept the religion of their rulers (which was more or less the terms on which the Thirty Years' War actually ended).

Its best English historian, C. V. Wedgwood, wrote of it that the war "need not have happened and settled nothing worth settling . . . The dismal course of the conflict, dragging on from one decade to the next and from one deadlock to the next, seems to me an object lesson on the dangers and disasters which can arise when men of narrow hearts and little minds are in high places."

By the eighteenth century there was a reaction against the horrors of such war. Fighting continued after the Westphalian Settlement, but within limits, meant to achieve reasonable political and dynastic purposes. The Italian historian Guglielmo Ferrero writes that "a formula for resolving conflicts between states [had by then been arrived at] that consisted in a mixture of war, negotiation, battles and indemnities . . ." He concludes, "Force can only serve [mankind] when it knows where to stop, for in intensifying itself it causes its own destruction. This is one of the simplest and most difficult of truths, and one which the human mind is both capable and yet incapable of comprehending."

The French Revolution ended this eighteenth-century interval of limited and instrumental war. Ferrero continues:

> At the end of the eighteenth century, an historical
> convulsion threw France into confusion and brought
> to power a generation of men full of energy but

without experience, strangers to the tradition of wisdom which had revealed to those who governed before them certain limits beyond which force was of
no avail. The young revolutionaries embarked on a
bold adventure, full of danger, during which, at a
certain moment, they were seized by fear; and im-
pelled by fear, they over-stepped the limits which
their predecessors had learned to respect. If the
Revolution did much evil, the reason was that at a
certain moment it was afraid of itself and of the
world. And in the madness of fear it believed it had
discovered a new art of warfare, a new diplomacy, a
new policy which were nothing but illusions about
the power of force . . . to oblige men to be free by
force. It might be possible to compel them by force
to *say* that they are free, but not by force to *be,* that is
to say to *feel* free. If any principle of legitimacy is
only valid in so far as it succeeds in obtaining the in-
ner consent, the sincere adherence, the spontaneous
impulse of the will, the principle of the sovereignty
of the people is completely identified with free consent . . . [With this choice by the revolutionaries
of] metaphysical adventure a new torment came to
afflict humanity . . . [From it] Fascism, Nazism, Bolshevism have all sprung.[5]

MAINSTREAM WESTERN THOUGHT in the nineteenth century
usually expressed confidence in the application of impartial
reason and the progress of science. Educated opinion was

that which Isaiah Berlin has attributed to the nineteenth-century Russian literary intelligentsia, that "solutions to all the central problems existed, that one could discover them, and, with sufficient selfless effort, realize them on earth." There already had been a number of utopian proposals and experiments for reordering society, including those of the utopian socialists, followed by the one that would prove the most important, Marx's dialectical and "scientific" interpretation of history, the basis for intensive political activity on the continent before 1918, as well as the rationale for the revolutionary uprising in Russia of the Bolsheviks led by Lenin.

Liberal confidence was destroyed in the general moral, social, and material catastrophe of the First World War. Afterward, the Europeans in 1919 turned to Woodrow Wilson and the United States with near-hysterical enthusiasm because the United States had stood apart from the revolutionary nineteenth century and had not been implicated in the war until its final months, when it was credited with bringing it to an end—even by the Germans and Austrians, who knew they could not be expected to stand against the millions of men the United States was calling to arms. This permitted both the Allied peoples and those of the Central Powers to believe that America might provide the rational and lasting solutions Wilson promised. They were unfortunately mistaken.

Karl Marx provided the nineteenth and twentieth centuries' most influential sociopolitical theory about past and future, with his account of man as divided into classes with conflicting interests, whose dialectical struggle would eventually empower the most progressive class, the working class. It was a rationale for twentieth-century revolution in Russia, after defeat by Japan in 1904 and humiliation by the Central Powers in the First World War. It was one of the motives for revolt, or left-wing or right-wing coups d'état, in interwar Europe and China, and it sustained movements of national affirmation and social protest in Africa, Asia, and Latin America in the postcolonial period. It survives today as an analytic tool and an influence on social democratic and revolutionary thought, and even on literary criticism.

Romanticism was the most important and consequential political force of the first half of the nineteenth century, following the Enlightenment, a challenge to Enlightenment rationalism, celebrating nature's authenticity and emphasizing feeling and emotion as more important to human fulfillment than bloodless reason. Romanticism was of German origin and was one of the sources of the developing nationalism in Europe as feudal institutions and dynastic power faded. Nationalism, an expression of community identity and felt destiny, became the most powerful political force in most of Europe during the post-Napoleonic period, and the most influential enemy of Enlightenment values. It was the main force destroying the Austro-Hungarian and Ottoman empires and influencing the rise of Fascism and National Socialism. The most remarkable achievement of the European Union since the Second World War has been to overcome nationalism among its own members, although it survives, sometimes virulently, in Balkan Europe and in the states that in the past were part of the Russian and Soviet empires.*

THE SEARCH FOR a secular utopian solution resumed after the First World War with Benito Mussolini, editor of a highly successful Socialist popular newspaper, who invented the term "totalitarian" to describe the commitment demanded by his inspired combination of socialism with nationalism in a new political party. In Italian Fascism the initial ideology was Mussolini's alliance of war veterans with workers in a party that broke the rules of the Italian system, brutalized and tortured its opponents, and proclaimed an imperial ambition. He was a charismatic figure, had actually been to war, served in an elite unit, had been decorated, and subsequently conducted himself as a hero, although as Luigi Barzini has said, when the new war he wanted actually came, his preparations and his bluster both proved empty.[6]

In the Nazi case, which unlike Italian Fascism was racist from the start, domination was by a self-identified racial elite. Nazi military aggression in the 1940s, and the Nazi party's defiance of the established rules of diplomacy and war and of existing treaties and international conventions on torture and treatment of prisoners and noncombatants (in the be-

---

* The irresponsible Western policy of pushing invitations to NATO onto Ukraine and Georgia stimulated destructive forces in those countries, and in Russia as well, by seeming to promise Western military support for irredentist or separatist ambitions that—as a reckless Georgian regime discovered in August 2008—would never actually be supplied.

ginning mainly, but not exclusively, violated in Central Europe and on the Eastern Front), together with its attempt to exterminate the Jews, among other peoples deemed inferior or corrupt, demonstrated Nazi contempt for European civilization. Nazism could not expect to universalize its values because these were by definition the natural and exclusive possessions of the Nordic ("Aryan") peoples, so while Scandinavians, the Dutch, and certain other groups could be admitted to full membership in the Nazi order, it subordinated "lesser" peoples to the status of serfs or set out to exterminate them as obstacles to a Nordic empire.

Hitler was also a decorated war veteran and possessor of charismatic powers, as was true of Leon Trotsky, an agitator, writer, and journalist. Trotsky proved a remarkable military organizer, creating the Red Army that defeated the Allied intervention in Russia of 1918–1920. Stalin had him murdered as a rival in 1940.*

The followers of the modern totalitarian leaders can scarcely be called the "marginal" people Norman Cohn found in the medieval movements. We have become aware of the ordinariness of most of the totalitarian parties' officials and members, and even of those implicated in Nazi and Leninist-Stalinist crimes. Much evil was done by soldiers or mobilized police who in peacetime would never have dreamed of carrying out orders of mass murder, but under

---

* The influence of Trotsky's doctrine of perpetual revolution persists to the present day. Most of the original American neoconservatives were of Trotskyist political (or even family) descent, so that his utopian and absolutist thinking influenced both the Bush administration's "war on terror" and Israeli right-wing extremism.

the discipline and social pressures of war obediently did so, sometimes even keeping photos or other souvenirs. Many villagers obediently killed their Jewish neighbors simply because they were told to do so. The same was true four decades later in the wars of Yugoslav succession, when Serbs and Croats fell upon one another, or on the Bosnian Muslims, for no reason except that such had become the thing to do as a consequence of the Serbian determination to create a "greater Serbia." In Rwanda, ethnic-linked class, power, and historical issues were being revenged.

WE ARE LEFT with the important question of the susceptibility of modern and enlightened people, not at all marginal, Asian as well as European and American, to the appeal of the secular utopian ideas of Fascism, Marxism, or of Pol Pot and his followers, or to accept the Maoism of the Cultural Revolution, believing in its "boundless, millenarian" promises.

We know from much personal and biographical testimony and experience that between the founding of the First International in 1864 and the Communist International in 1919, to the end of Soviet Communism in 1991, uncounted numbers of well-meaning people, including many intellectuals, artists, and academic figures, voluntarily accepted party discipline, suppressed their doubts, committed crimes, and engaged in clandestine struggles and conspiracies that in the end proved merely to have aggrandized the power of the leaders of totalitarian parties.

The attack on the established international order by Leninist Russia, its creation of the Comintern (the Communist

International, controlled by the Soviet Communist Party), and its sponsorship of foreign Communist parties intent on subversion and overthrow of other governments, together with the criminal practices of Stalinism in controlling Soviet and Soviet-dominated societies, demonstrated one lesson about modern secular utopianism that must not be lost: Ruthlessness is seductive, perhaps particularly to intellectuals convinced that they see the future and therefore are licensed to sacrifice to it vast numbers of unimportant people (in military terms, "cannon fodder").

The willingness of Communist Party members and fellow travelers to submit themselves to Party discipline rested upon their confidence (or secular religious faith, to be exact) that Marxism was indeed an objective scientific account of society and its future, which it was not—as should have been apparent to serious people from the start. The notion of an eventual proletarian age in which the apparatus of state would fall away while "a new type of man" created by Socialism (and its "towering leaders") would live in permanent harmony with his fellows could only be accepted through the deliberate suppression of the critical faculties of any Communist adherent with experience of political society or any knowledge of history.

As with Nazism, self-intoxication was everywhere. Hundreds of thousands of intelligent people went to Communism "as to a spring of fresh water" (as Picasso said). Arthur Koestler, author of *Darkness at Noon*, said Communism rescued him "from inauthenticity"; he was "thirsting for faith"; he "felt the jubilant exaltation of being free" the day he joined the German Communist Party. Thoughtful people had always been willing to believe in a heaven located in heaven, but since the beginning of the secular age, all too many of them have been glad to believe in the possibility of heaven on earth.[7]

This was possible within a new Western intellectual and moral structure that rested wholly on faith in science and secular progress. Peter Gay was correct to call ours an age of the Modern Paganism, since the period has been dominated by the aggressively pagan ideologies of dialectical material-ism, Bolshevism, racism, an ultimately nihilistic Nazism, and Maoism—to take the major ones; although one must add a nihilistic capitalism.

THE DRAMA IN the contemporary Middle East is usually thought to be linked to religious fanaticism, in turn associ-ated with totalitarian thought. Few, in the United States at least, are accustomed to see jihadism as a political phenomenon—a defense of religious and cultural identity against hostile foreign influence, which is a version of "nationalism." Yet terrorism involving Muslims made its appearance in contemporary history as a reaction to West-ern political (or imperial) interference in the Middle East. Palestinian bombings and hijackings began as resistance to Israel. Israel's creation itself was preceded by both Zionist and Arab terrorism during the 1930s and 1940s, most of the Zionist attacks being directed against the British as the mandatory authority. Terrorist attacks by Muslims have widely been interpreted as irrational, seemingly senseless or gratuitous acts because in many cases they are suicidal and they kill innocent individuals, including fellow Muslims and even sympathizers, as well as people believed infidels and the enemies of Islam. But Osama bin Laden himself identified the U.S. military presence in the Middle East as the motive for al Qaeda's suicidal attacks against the United States in 2001—attacks that were deliberate blows against symbols in New York and Washington of Western capitalism and militarism. The attacks were meant as revenge for the presence of "infidel" American bases in the holy land of Saudi Arabia.

Attacks on American or other foreign soldiers in Lebanon or Iraq or Afghanistan are described by those responsible as attacks on "occupiers" or intruders, and Hizbollah and Hamas terrorism attacks Israeli annexation of Palestinian lands as well as the very existence of the state of Israel in the Middle East. While the religio-political utopianism of today's radical Islam includes certain features of the religious fanaticism of the past, notably in its view of martyrdom, it is actually a modern phenomenon in that its purpose is political, to create a grand union of integrist Muslims to oppose heresy in the Islamic world, and to oppose foreign cultural influence and military invasion. Like the Zionism and Jewish nationalism of the nineteenth and twentieth centuries, committed to creating a Jewish homeland, the utopian Islamic society the radicals promise would exist in this world, not the next. It is one more version of modern utopian nationalism—which in the United States of America has meanwhile assumed a wholly different form.

III

The Sources of America's Moral and Political Isolation from Europe

I<small>T IS IMPOSSIBLE FULLY TO UNDERSTAND</small> the predicament of the American and Western political situation today without placing it in the context of the entire period that began with the European discoveries of the Americas and their indigenous societies. This was followed by the Enlightenment, and the related and contingent foundation of the United States by the British North American colonists, unwilling to continue to live as British subjects lacking full parliamentary representation. These Americans escaped the principal cultural consequence of the Enlightenment that was producing among European elites a crisis of established religion, and what might be described as a revolution in eschatological expectation, and hence in confidence in the established nature of political society.

The full meaning of the American Declaration of Independence was its "declaration" of a new, separate, and self-sufficient manifestation of Western civilization in the supposedly innocent territories of North America, a step not taken by Spanish and French colonists.* The customary citation of John Winthrop's identification of America as a divinely provided refuge for English Protestant dissidents has led to a popular disregard of the political and secular intellectual forces that went into the new republic's creation, which was seen as indeed providing man's "last, best hope" as a new political dispensation replacing the monarchical order of Europe. As Thomas Paine put it in *The Rights of Man*, "the case and circumstances of America present themselves as in the beginning of the world . . . We have no occasion to roam for information in the obscure field of antiquity nor hazard ourselves upon conjecture. We are . . . as if we had lived in the beginning of time."

The counsel originally drawn from this was that the new nation should keep a safe distance from the affairs of Europe, then considered (as often remains the case today in the United States) an exhausted society and source of political and moral corruption. The nation followed the prudent advice of George Washington in 1796: to avoid permanent alliances with the European states ("entangling" alliances, as Jefferson added in his first inaugural address). The advice was generally respected during the century and a half following the nation's foundation, reinforced by the

---

* The independence movement in the Latin American colonies did not begin until two decades later, and there are those who argue that, with respect to the overlordship of the United States, it has yet to be completed. Canada did not become a united nation in spirit until the Battle of Vimy Ridge in April 1917, when the four separate divisions of the Canadian Expeditionary Force for the first time fought as a Canadian army.

Monroe Doctrine, which opposed any further European intervention in the Americas.

From the beginning, Europeans and others had been imaginatively and morally gripped by the American national adventure, seeing in it the same universal importance Americans attributed to their nation and national example, as a republican political and egalitarian social experiment, a decisive departure from the Western past. This awareness was religious for the Puritans who settled Massachusetts and Connecticut, but more than a century later it was also implicit in the exalted language and noble sentiments of the Declaration of Independence and the Constitution. The United States became unique among nations as one that created itself consciously, as a new beginning.

THE SOLOMON R. GUGGENHEIM Museum in New York City, in association with the Royal Academy of Arts in London and the Louvre and the Galeries Nationales du Grand-Palais in Paris, presented a remarkable exhibition during 2006–2007 called "Public and Private Portraits 1770–1830." It assembled sixty years of human portraits in Europe and the United States during a period when portraiture abandoned the convention that portrait painting concerned only rulers and the eminent in society, serving only political and monumental purposes. The period 1770 to 1830 was one of great cultural as well as political significance, that of post-Enlightenment and revolutionary consciousness, with the emergence of the United States signifying the arrival of a society consciously set on replacing the established European order.

This claim was asserted in the exhibition's hanging, which deliberately confronted "old" Europe with new America. On one side of the gallery (in Paris, where I saw the exhibition) formal paintings were hung of the European monarchs, Louis XVI, George III, Ferdinand VII of Spain, and Pope Pius VII, all displayed with the accoutrements and conventional symbols of power, status, and remoteness: the pope on his throne, wearing the Ring of Peter; Ferdinand in royal costume with his orders, royal baton in his hand; George III similarly attired (the last British monarch whose titles included monarch of Great Britain and Ireland, Elector of Hanover, and the yet to be renounced British royal family's claim to the throne of France), wearing an ermine robe, crown and a scepter beside him.

In sober contrast was a Gilbert Stuart standing portrait (formerly hung in the New York Public Library) of George Washington in a plain black suit with the sheathed sword of a former general. His hand touches a document on the table next to him, and a small republican shield ornaments the chair. Next to it was a Houdon bust, in Roman style, of Benjamin Franklin in plain coat and cravat, and a painting (commissioned by John Hancock from John Singleton Copley) of Samuel Adams, plainly dressed in a gentleman's suit, as he pleaded the case of the colonists to the British governor following the Boston Massacre of March 1770.

The radical discontinuity, the caesura in the procession of Western civilization, is clearly indicated. The society of order, rank, and hierarchical religion that had lasted from before the Roman period to the fantastical seventeenth- and eighteenth-century European refinement of the trappings of monarchical power, empire, and inherited privilege had been broken. A new society of democratic order, merit, humane values, and earned distinction and service had made its appearance and, as the visitor to the exhibition was meant to understand, would triumph. The exhibition of that triumph in the year 2007 in the three symbolic cities of contemporary Western modernity—Paris, London, and New York—inevitably provoked reflection on the significance today of what then was understood as the succession of American simplicity and virtue to Europe's display and pretension.

The exhibition provided social and political confirmation of another, equally significant and fateful mutation in the Western historical consciousness which had been presented in an earlier exhibition on the occasion of the American bicentennial mounted by the Cleveland Museum of Art, called "The European Vision of America," that was also shown internationally to much attention.[1] It displayed the revelation of the American continent and its indigenous civilizations to the Europeans in the centuries of discovery as an incitement to the radical reexamination and intellectual reconstruction of Europe itself in the seventeenth- and eighteenth-century Enlightenment. It dealt with a succession of European fantasies assuming an American Eden populated by innocent and exotic native peoples, suggesting the original world of mankind. This was a fantasy inspiring speculation that America's discovery might make possible a human recreation of lost innocence, in a land of unimaginably beautiful and implausible flora and fauna, Another Place. It suggested, as well, the possibility of the redemption and relaunch of human history.

Here, too, the exhibition presented contemporary

European portraits of Washington and Franklin (the latter by Fragonard, "Le docteur Franklin crowned by Liberty" [1778]), as well as plates, candelabras, medals, and tapestries commemorating the foundation of the United States, classically virtuous and self-governing, an example to Europe of what the future might offer.

IN THE EIGHTEENTH and early nineteenth centuries, only a narrow North American elite was part of the Enlightenment intellectual upheaval, experiencing its influence in the same way as Western Europe. The intellectual life of the United States in the colonial and federal periods was dominated by religious influences, despite the contrary impression given by the profundity and elegance of the nation's founders' published debates on the institutions of the new republic and their philosophies of government.

This transatlantic cultural difference offers an explanation for the phenomenal confidence of Americans over many generations in "the American system," and their unwillingness to contemplate basic constitutional change. It helps to explain the exceptional and detached role the United States assumed in international affairs, and chiefly those of Western Europe. The conventional interpretation of the Enlightenment is that it constituted humanity's "coming of age." This meant a divorce from divine help and divine hope—a profound cultural mutation with dramatic political consequences, which geographically isolated North America did not share. America from the start was "God's own country," assumed to be a finished foundation, part of God's fixed plan.

The United States was in the revolutionary and federal periods the undoubted scene of the great political achievement of the Enlightenment, the creation of the American republic, but the intellectual forces of Scottish and English philosophy were as important as those of France, even though today Benjamin Franklin and Thomas Jefferson are in France considered among the *philosophes* of the age. The Enlightenment, however, failed to produce a stable political result in Europe; instead, violent overthrow of the dynastic and hereditary system followed, and an incompletely achieved counter-revolution after Napoleon's defeat. The United States in the same period had successfully established the constitutional representative republic that exists today.

With America's escape from social revolution, and general rejection of Enlightenment paganism, the Enlightenment assumed different forms and produced different results on the two sides of the Atlantic. In doing so it confirmed the righteous view Americans have since held of themselves as free from continental European tendencies toward "extremist" politics, and instead as exemplars (and saviors) of democracy—humanity's Next Step.

The landowners, farmers, professional men, and militia officers of British North America, under the conservative influences of British constitutionalism and common law, demonstrated that (with the military assistance of Bourbon France!) the old order could be replaced with a new one of representative and republican government, a society of democratic assumptions, manners, and individual responsibility. (To say this requires ignoring—as the founding fathers uneasily did—the continued institution of slavery in the new United States.) It was to learn about this achievement and describe it to his countrymen that Alexis de Tocqueville later wrote his great book *Democracy in America*.

THE ENLIGHTENMENT ATTACK on established religion and the French Revolution had deeply negative effects on the eighteenth-century American mind. The French Revolution "burst forth like a volcano," the American Presbyterian churchman Robert Baird wrote, "and threatened to sweep the United States into its fiery stream." From 1790 to 1815, according to Perry Miller, Harvard's eminent intellectual historian of the period, "an immense . . . literature [was written] of denunciation of the French Revolution, with proportionately nearly nothing on its behalf." Miller says that the great wave of evangelical Protestant religious revivalism that occurred in America in the decades preceding and following the Revolution had little to do with continental European events. It was largely a local American religious undertaking, to rescue the United States "from a spiritual deterioration hardly to be equaled in the darkest chapters of Christian history," produced by the sins and iniquities of America (those of France were ignored), these being, as militant Methodists identified them, "our growing idolatry, which is covetousness and the prevailing love of the world," manifested in "profanation of the Sabbath, disobedience of parents, and increase of drunkenness." The American version of "the magnificent era of revivals inaugurated in or around 1800 [in England] . . . was in great part an internal convulsion, and it progressively endeavored to conceive of itself as exclusively internal."[2]

The religious historian Mark A. Noll has consistently argued against the idea that there was from the beginning "a Christian America," with specifically Protestant Christian influences at work to make American institutions what they have become today. This has been a popular notion among the Protestant religious right in recent years, the supposed Christian inspiration for American democracy having become an important part of conservative (and Republican Party) arguments concerning the origins of the United States and its form of government, part of the electoral argument that "liberals" have repudiated America's cultural and religious legacy.* Noll says the origin of the United States was a notably secular event conducted (he quotes Ralph C. Wood of [Baptist] Baylor University) "by deistic Episcopalians who believed neither in original sin nor in Israel and Christ as God's unique provisions for the world's salvation."[3] When, at the Constitutional Convention, Benjamin Franklin moved the assembly to a prayer to God, the motion did not pass.

NEW ENGLAND WAS the location of the most influential American literary and philosophical culture of the eighteenth and early nineteenth centuries, that of "ministers and pedants," as the late literary critic Alfred Kazin has said.[4] The agrarian South remained under the cultural and literary influences of England and Scotland, where its commercial ties

---

* In 2007 there was a proposal (unsuccessful) in Congress for legislation rewriting the history of the period to affirm evangelical Protestant religious inspiration for the Constitution.

were greatest. The coastal and plantation "Cavalier" South was marked by the romantic royalism of the English Civil War, which had American repercussions. Illusions of the Southern elite's class and cultural superiority (product of "the diseased imagination" of Southerners, according to Gideon Welles, who was to become Union Secretary of the Navy) were greatly exaggerated at the time of the Civil War, with mostly disastrous effect for the South, lasting well after the burning of Atlanta by General William Tecumseh Sherman in 1864 and the collapse of the Confederacy.[5] The most important literary figure of the antebellum South was Edgar Allan Poe, and with him the transatlantic influence was west to east, with Poe's eventual considerable effect upon the French Symbolists.

In New England, by the mid-1830s, the founding Calvinist Puritanism, and the denominational innovations and divisions that followed, gave way to the individualist rationalism of Unitarianism, subsequently reinterpreted for Americans by Ralph Waldo Emerson and Theodore Parker as a religion of natural reason and conscience, belief in innate human goodness, and universal salvation. Its literary and philosophical counterpart was Transcendentalism, affirming the inherent divinity of nature as well as man, and holding that the highest source of knowledge is individual intuition, rejecting traditional authority.

The Transcendentalists were particularly influenced by Emmanuel Kant, the German Romantics, and by William Wordsworth, Thomas Carlyle, and Samuel Taylor Coleridge. The movement began among a group of friends in Boston and Concord, and was to influence most major American writers of the time: Nathaniel Hawthorne, Herman Melville, Walt Whitman, Henry David Thoreau, Margaret Fuller (and Louisa May Alcott and her immortal *Little Women*). The Transcendentalists published the influential journal *The Dial* and inspired the Brook Farm cooperative social reform experiment.

Transcendentalism lives on in the American consciousness (or subconscious). It held that man finds divinity in himself, and that progress is inevitable, two enduring pillars of American national complacency. Its decisive development came when Emerson left the Unitarian ministry in 1834 and began his phenomenal career as American seer, inspirer, and enthusiastic preacher—although Kazin describes him as "blandness itself" on the lecture platform, with "ideas not original enough to make him a philosopher," but good enough to make him the most influential essayist and lecturer of his day in America, promising that the past was dead and the future of America uniquely bright. His self-satisfied Phi Beta Kappa address at Harvard in 1837, "The American Scholar," was enormously influential and is anthologized even today.*

Emerson's undemanding and self-reassuring religion of optimism became one of the distinguishing strains in American thought, inspiring best-selling books of religious reassurance that continue to appear, entering into incongruous civil unions

---

* Kazin also quotes Tolstoy's note, written during the Crimean War: "A conversation about Divinity and Faith has suggested to me a great, stupendous idea, to the realization of which I feel capable of devoting my life. That idea is the founding of a new religion corresponding to the present stage of mankind: the religion of Christ but purged of dogmas and absolutism—a practical religion, not promising future bliss but giving bliss on earth." Emerson anticipated him.

with the popular psychology of self-realization and main-stream, quasi-fundamentalist evangelicalism—itself originally a poor man's religion, which Transcendentalism certainly was not. This eventually gave birth to the late-twentieth-century phenomenon of suburban Pentecostal mega-churches that preach prosperity as evidence of virtue, and an all-embracing and uncritical God of American nationality.

It took Charles Darwin, not the Enlightenment, to shake American religious and cultural complacency and isolation. Evolution became and remains to the present day an issue in American presidential politics as well as in American public education (where school-board battles over teaching Darwin-ism persist). The great Middle Western populist reformer and unshakable fundamentalist believer William Jennings Bryan, who was the unsuccessful Democratic presidential candidate in 1896, 1900, and 1908, and later Woodrow Wilson's secretary of state (resigning on principle when American entered the First World War), was ruined by the controversy over Darwinism.[6]

It seems fair to say that most American churchgoers from the eighteenth to the beginning of the twentieth century (and by and large, the religiously disposed or questing unchurched as well) have been opposed to what most Europeans considered fundamental tenets of the Enlightenment.

SERIOUS LITERARY AND cultural relations with Europe in the later nineteenth and early twentieth centuries took the form of American elite expatriation, as in the cases of Henry Adams (descendant of presidents, the author of a classic reflection on *Mont-Saint-Michel and Chartres,* who returned to Washington, D.C., to write an influential and disabused fictional account of American politics, *Democracy*), and the novelists Henry James and Edith Wharton. Their preoccupation was the American confrontation with European civilization and worldliness, a social issue as much as a cultural one. Henry James, in his 1878 novel *The Europeans,* has one of his Europeanized American protagonists tell his sister, after a trip to the United States to meet their Boston cousins: "What are they like . . . ? Like nothing you ever saw. They are sober; they are even severe. They are of a pensive cast; they take things hard. I think there is something the matter with them; they have some melancholy memory or some depressing expectation. It's not the Epicurian temperament."

"Christian America," meaning Protestant America, was the ultimate outcome of the decline of a pitiless New England Calvinism by way of Transcendentalism and Emersonianism into the generally undemanding theology of the traditional Protestantism of America's upper classes. Episcopalianism, Presbyterianism, and Congregationalism were the well-to-do accompaniment to a lower-class Protestantism of the poor whose religion came from the great evangelical revivals that began in Britain, and to the rapid spread in America of Methodist evangelism and eventual Baptist adherence. The "Holiness" current in Methodism, Pentecostal in character, took root in the United States and became a crucial element in the rise of popular Protestant fundamentalism.

This is the American form of Protestant Christianity that has since become the dominant popular religion, its pattern of devotion and action constant since the eighteenth century.

The individual recognizes the inerrancy of the Bible, affirms in public his past sinfulness and faith in salvation through belief in Jesus Christ, testifies that he or she has emotionally experienced the transformation of being "born again," and is then welcomed into the community of the saved.

The religion of the poor white South, Calvinist and evangelical, committed to private interpretation of the scripture and individual justification through personal encounters with the Savior (hence: "finding Jesus," an avowal most ambitious American politicians even today find essential), was shaped by the thought of the Dutch theologian Jacobus Arminius (1560–1609), who influenced Charles and John Wesley and thus American Protestantism. He argued that "irresistible grace" was compatible with men's achieving their own good through hard work, frugality, and consequent material success: thus the American Protestant association of riches and success with virtue, as visible signs of "election."

This religion was faithful to the literal interpretation of the King James English translation of the Bible—particularly the Old Testament—that for many years (often through oral transmission) was the most important cultural force at work in a largely illiterate or poorly educated population. (A late-nineteenth-century Texas governor banned teaching foreign languages in Texas schools, saying that "English was good enough for Jesus.")

Much of the Southern population was of "Scotch-Irish" origin, Calvinist predestinarian Protestants, first implanted in Northern Ireland by Britain in the seventeenth century by James I, as part of his effort to control or replace the original Catholic Irish population. In the eighteenth and nineteenth centuries, many of the Scotch-Irish emigrated to North America and had a great influence on the white culture of the American South, that of free yeoman farmers. Their individualism, intolerant religion, and, usually, their poverty were much more important in forming the lasting Southern "national character" than the Anglo-Irish romantic and aristocratic influences of the same period, cultivated by the prosperous in the plantation South, where large properties could be given over to slave-cultivated cotton production.

The Scotch-Irish were also marked by their descendance from a premodern clan tradition where personal and collective honor, pride, and vengeance were important. Hence the fairly high incidence of casual violence and family feuds in the South, particularly in its Appalachian mountain communities, which remained largely untouched by urban development for many years after the Civil War, until the Second World War and even after. Folkways, music, religion, and language displayed certain sixteenth- and seventeenth-century characteristics into contemporary times.*

THIS SOUTHERN LEGACY has contributed to the global reputation of the United States for a popular culture of violence

---

* This writer was a soldier in a largely Southern infantry unit of the U.S. Army in 1951–1952, where Elizabethan turns of phrase were not uncommon in the ordinary usage of white soldiers from rural Appalachia, such as speaking of "frolic" to mean celebration while on weekend passes, or the use of "yon" to indicate direction. Southern country music has old sources in Scottish and English folk music. By now it has become commercialized mainstream music, although recognizable for what it was and where it began.

unknown anywhere in Western Europe, usually associated primarily with the frontier experience. The push westward toward a receding frontier, the conquest of the aboriginal American population and their displacement by European settlers who considered Indian land "unoccupied," open to appropriation and the installation of "civilization," was for nearly a century identified as the crucial historical influence on the development of the American nation and American democracy, a thesis first set out by Frederick Jackson Turner in 1893—although in the politically corrected twenty-first century it has lost some of the self-congratulatory luster it originally possessed.

The initial North American experience superficially resembled that of the Spanish conquest and occupation of South and Central America, except that nowhere in North America were there (surviving?) indigenous civilizations of the sophistication of those encountered by the Spanish. By and large, the North American settlers (except in Quebec) lacked the Spanish and Portuguese religious motivation, to save the souls of the pagan Indians (as well as to find Eldorado).

The North Americans' was a violent and brief conquest of the West. The Union Pacific Railroad was chartered by Congress in 1862 to build the eastern part of the transcontinental railroad, and construction began in 1865 on a line from Council Bluffs, Iowa, on the Missouri River, to Ogden, Utah. That opened the free-range West to land-grant occupation and settlement, cattle drives and cattle wars, Billy the Kid, the dime novel, Owen Wister, Zane Gray—and, ultimately, John Wayne. Thirty years later the "Old West" was over, except in the newly invented movies. The last known "wild" Indian was captured in California early in the twentieth century and was taken in hand by university researchers. Nonetheless, the experience of "the conquest of the West" dominated the American imagination for many years, and it persists today. My own great-uncle slept with a Colt .45 "Peacemaker" revolver under his pillow in the 1930s, in a town that had ceased to be the frontier sixty years earlier. My grandfather (born in 1862) carved for me as a child a bow and arrows as he had been taught by a "tame" Indian. Today, in an American society that is more violent than the Old West, the popular demand to possess and bear individual weapons continues to be politically irresistible—more than ever, it appears, since the 2008 presidential election.

The South was violent for another reason. It was a slave-holding society, where plantation discipline was maintained by the threat or practice of violence, and poor whites in Southern communities struggled to maintain a status superior to that of slaves, even though their material conditions of life were sometimes inferior to those of the slaves on a prosperous plantation. After Emancipation, the living condition of the "red-neck" (a reference to sunburn) white farmer "share-cropping" for a more prosperous farmer or landowner was usually no better than that of the black who shared that miserable condition.

Vigilante "law" and lynching were supported in places where organized law enforcement was weak or absent.

Vigilante groups, usually composed of the respectable, originally mostly found their victims among white criminals or
supposed law-breakers, since slaves were valuable property
and were expected to be controlled by their owners. Lynching as an instrument of racist oppression of free blacks was
a post-Emancipation phenomenon in the so-called "Jim
Crow" period at the end of the nineteenth century and the
first half of the twentieth (often in supposed crimes of sex-
ual connotation). The practice spread to Northern cities
with large immigrant and migrant black populations.* The
last lynchings were in the 1950s, but there were murders
of (usually white) civil rights activists in the South in the
1960s.

It has been argued that an American national deformity
results from its people never having known tragedy. But
that is to ignore the tragedy of slave life in North America
between 1619, when the first slaves were landed in North
America (from the British Bahamas), and Emancipation,
and the additional century of racial oppression of black
Americans that followed Emancipation. The music of black
America was from the start the music of suffering and
tragedy, and even when comic was sardonic and bitter. Jim
Crow persecution and widespread disenfranchisement of
blacks after Emancipation, effectively nullifying it in most
of the Old South, found an eventual amelioration in President Harry Truman's courageous and deeply important

---

* In the 1920s and 1930s there was a notable rise of Ku Klux Klan activity in the Midwest, in this case anti-Catholic and anti-immigrant as
  well as racial.

desegregation of the American military services in 1948.* It took another twenty years to arrive at the civil rights legislation of Lyndon Johnson, and forty years more before the election of Barack Obama.

Tragedy was a related reality in the experience of the white population of the morally compromised slaveholding South, and after 1865 the conquered white South, whose literature in the generations that followed what it called the War Between the States was deeply marked by defeat and even more by the continuing reality and legacy of its complicity in slavery and Jim Crow in all their human ramifications. William Faulkner was the great chronicler of this period. It could be felt in the former Confederate states as late as the 1960s, when the changes in American economic and industrial geography that had begun during the Second World War, and its accompanying labor mobility, plus the influence of national radio broadcasting and above all of television, were accomplishing a national fusion of popular culture and attitudes that by now has all but extinguished

---

* The army obediently desegregated and became the most important vehicle of black male social and professional ascension the United States has ever had, a role that continues. The U.S. Navy and Marine Corps, "gentlemen's" services, resisted, so long as their officer corps were able to do so. The only desegregation the navy wanted was black labor and construction units plus its old practice of employing black or Filipino stewards in officers' messes. The Marines stayed all-white, or nearly so, longer, pleading that their supposedly unique fighting qualities depended on an enlisted corps that was a "band of brothers." The army had always been culturally a Southern institution, meaning that in ordinary life blacks and whites mingled despite segregated institutions, which actually made it easier for the army to accept racial desegregation, even in the ranks.

the authenticity of regional cultures in the United States, although not of regional differences.

IT HAS BEEN said of America's Evangelical Protestants that "instead of creating a Christian America as was their initial intention, . . . [they] have effectively Americanized Christianity." Their belief is a fundamentalist, interdenominational or multidenominational Pentecostal Christianity that is an American invention (or amalgamation), far from its roots in dissenting Anglicanism, Calvinism, the influences of Moravian piety, and the theology of Jacobus Arminius. David Hempton wrote in the *Times Literary Supplement* in 2007 that the movement has "at once condemned, appropriated and consumed popular culture [which helps to explain] the paradox that has befuddled secularization theorists for years of how modern America has become more religious and more secular at the same time."[7]

While the movement is properly called an American version of Christianity, it has failed to convert the American majority to its version of Christianity. The overall average of Sunday churchgoers in the United States may be higher than in Western Europe, but urban, educated, professional, and academic America, including the government policy class, is no less secular than its counterparts abroad—although politicians of Protestant origin usually find it expedient to acknowledge religion's conventions and declare themselves "saved." Evangelicals faithfully attend church, but so do Catholic Latinos, the most rapidly growing demographic group in the United States.

The international political significance of the rise of the American Evangelicals lies in its adherents' passionate conviction that the United States is God's chosen instrument in his salvation plan, and their identification of their religious expectations with the events of contemporary history, looking for signs that predicted redemptive events are at hand. A great many are convinced that the great Middle Eastern ally of the United States, Israel, is crucial to the fulfillment of the divine plan, having carried out that return of the Jews to Jerusalem described as indispensable to the fulfillment of the predicted Last Days and the end of time, when "saved" Christians and those Jews who have chosen conversion will welcome the final apocalyptic battles with the Evil One and the arrival of the Christian redeemer.

The Evangelicals have made a special and not unsuccessful effort to win military converts. The moral tension between Christian commitment and a career commitment to the employment of state violence is surely eased if one believes this participates in events of divine significance. Since early in the development of the American all-volunteer professional military service, Evangelical clergymen have figured disproportionately among the candidates for appointment to the military chaplains' corps. While military regulations are rigorous in defining permitted religious activity and proselytism, there have been scandals in this connection, the most notorious being that at the Air Force Academy in

Colorado (which trains secondary-school graduates to become career officers). Nonbelievers, Catholics, and Jewish and mainstream Protestant cadets have complained of academic or professional discrimination and aggressive proselytism tacitly encouraged by senior officers who are themselves committed Evangelicals, prompting official investigations.

Certain officers prominent in the Pentagon during the George W. Bush administration publicly identified the war in Iraq as a divine commission to the United States. Mr. Bush's own avowed Evangelical commitment has provoked questions in some quarters about his motives in his official decisions. In spring 2009 a friend of the retired president of the French Republic, Jacques Chirac, confided to a journalist friend preparing a book on Chirac's presidency that in 2003, just before the U.S. invasion of Iraq, Mr. Chirac was twice telephoned by President Bush, urging France to join the invasion because the world had arrived at the era prefigured by Gog and Magog, signifying the arrival of a great war in which all God's enemies would be destroyed and the Last Days of Divine Judgement arrive. Mr. Bush seemed convinced that his war on Iraq was this prophesied war, and tried to so convince Chirac. The French president was sufficiently disturbed by Bush's state of mind to consult a theologian at the University of Lausanne in Switzerland for his opinion. The theologian told him that Gog is a mysterious figure from the land of Magog, of controversial Biblical significance, mentioned in the book of Genesis and again in Ezekiel and Revelation, taken by

some to represent the nations of the world who are enemies of Israel at the end-time. The French president decided to keep the nature of these telephone conversations
to himself so long as he (and, as it happened, Mr. Bush)
remained in office.*

* Jean-Claude Maurice, *Si vous le répétez, je démentirai* (Paris: Plon, 2009).
The translation of the deliberately provocative title is "If you repeat
this, I'll deny it," but the book's information about the Bush calls has
been widely published in the French and other press and never has
been denied by Mr. Chirac.

IV

From American Isolationism to Utopian Interventionism

THE FUNCTION OF NATIONAL myth is to explain history and a nation's (and implicitly, the individual's) role therein. Underlying nearly everything said or written about history—in the West, at least, where the awareness first emerged of it as an intelligible or meaningful progression through time—there is an implicit belief that history has a meaning, and from that belief or assumption, a nation acts. This is true of the foreign policy of modern nations.

A belief in national election and mission was integral to the American identity during the first century and a half of the nation's history, but its effect was to emphasize the separateness of the American nation from the Europe from which nearly all of its people had come, and to validate a foreign policy that isolated the United States from the affairs of Europe, considered politically turbulent and potentially compromising, or ideologically contaminating.

With Woodrow Wilson, the national myth was turned into a philosophy of international action. The United States became convinced that it could provide a solution to the crisis that gripped Europe. Its national virtues would enable it to become the savior nation the world presumably awaited. The First World War's carnage and futility destroyed Europe's confidence in its civilization. The Europeans enthusiastically (to American gratification) welcomed American intervention in that war and Wilson's Fourteen Point Plan for peace. When Wilson arrived in Paris in 1919 it was to what witnesses described as near-hysterical popular enthusiasm.

With Wilson, a fundamental change had taken place in twentieth-century American thinking about world affairs. From the period of the French Revolution the new United States had mostly been spared the conflicts in European state relations. After the Congress of Vienna, which settled the Napoleonic legacy, these conflicts seemed to Americans a matter of those "jealousies and rivalries of the complicated politics of Europe" that Wilson and others were to condemn as the cause of the Great War.

From the time of the Barbary Pirates until the conversion of the United States to an idealistic imperialism in 1898 (seizing Spain's empire—for the good of its natives—in what became known in Spain as the Catastrophe), international affairs had not greatly perturbed Americans. Foreign relations all but exclusively concerned disputes connected with commerce or the continental expansion of the United States into territories belonging to or claimed by Britain, Canada, Russia, or Spain. France's possession of the Louisiana territories, between the Mississippi and the Rocky Mountains, was settled by Thomas Jefferson's purchase of them from Napoleon in 1803.

Besides confronting the resistance of the aboriginal peoples of what had become the United States, the citizens of the new nation fought and lost a second war with Britain in 1812 in an effort to expand into Canada (and had the British burn Washington in retaliation), but settled with the Spaniards in Florida in 1819 after the first Seminole War. After 1823 the British government found it convenient quietly to support the Monroe Doctrine, opposing any European presence or colonization in the Americas (notwithstanding a certain cautious subsequent interest by London in exploiting the existence of the Confederacy, so long as it survived).*

The United States otherwise faced no real threats from overseas, and threw its energies into the pursuit of its original conception of Manifest Destiny: transcontinental territorial expansion (and commerce). It annexed Mexican Texas and California, and all the territories between, by means of a white Texan declaration of independence and a war (1846–1847) in which Mexico was defeated, with Washington subsequently paying fifteen million dollars compensation for New Mexico and California, and assuming claims against the Mexican government.

The Civil War was the republic's first and last experience of a major war in which it suffered heavy casualties and attacks on civilian society. It was also, for reasons of technological development, the first truly modern war, an industrial

---

* Not everyone is aware that the Monroe Doctrine also renounced any United States role "in the wars of the European powers" or "in matters relating [to the European states]."

and railroad war, at least on the part of the Union. General Ulysses S. Grant's strategy, exemplified by William Tecumseh Sherman's "March Through Georgia" (from Chattanooga, Tennessee, to Atlanta and Savannah, and then northward through South Carolina to Goldsboro, North Carolina), destroying with its massive industrial supremacy the Confederacy's civilian agrarian economy, was to set a precedent for American military practice during the Second World War and the Korean War.

The war against Spain in 1898, however catastrophic for Spain, was for the United States a casual affair in which the nation itself was never seriously engaged elsewhere than in the Philippines, where it had to fight for three years against an independence movement whose leaders had mistakenly believed that the Americans had come to liberate them, and where the United States subsequently fought what would today be called a counterinsurgency war against Muslim "Moro" separatists in Mindanao that lasted until 1916. (That same war has resumed today, with American soldiers as advisers to Filipino troops, and the Moros awarded the new identity of Muslim terrorists.)

THE AMERICAN INTERVENTION in the First World War was an event of lasting consequence because of the meaning assigned to it by Woodrow Wilson, son and grandson of Presbyterian ministers, who during his years of eminence as a university president (Princeton), governor of New Jersey, and twenty-eighth president of the United States became convinced that the American nation, and he personally, were bearers of a divine commission to reform civilization by abolishing war and extending to the globe the benevolent principles of American democracy and religion.*

He believed that the world "will turn to America for those moral aspirations which lie at the basis of all freedom . . . that . . . all shall know that she puts human rights above all other rights, and that her flag is the flag not only of America, but of humanity."[1] He reinterpreted the world war as an ideological war, just as the wars of the French Revolution had been a century earlier wars meant to change the condition of humanity. The world war would be the war "that would end war," producing permanent peace. "[America's world role has come] by no plan of our conceiving, but by the hand of God who led us into this way . . . It was of this that we dreamed at our birth. America indeed shall in truth show the way." These were Wilson's words on July 10, 1919, in his address to the U.S. Senate presenting the peace treaty. Such claims surpassed historical possibility; but they subsequently became integral to the vocabulary and ambition of American national policy.

With Woodrow Wilson the Manifest Destiny of the

---

* Hailing the Chinese Revolution of 1911–1912, Wilson said this could be the most momentous event of the generation, and he considered that as a matter of course the American minister to China should be an Evangelical Christian so that China could be "made" both democratic and Christian, thus to exercise a stabilizing influence on Asian affairs—an ambition with a distinct Bush-administration ring. As quoted in Tang Tsou, *America's Failure in China, 1941–50* (Chicago: University of Chicago Press, 1963), 5. On Wilson's personal conviction, see Louis Anchincloss, *Woodrow Wilson* (New York: Viking, 2007), 44.

United States ceased to be continental expansion and national power and progress, and was reimagined as a divinely ordained mission to humanity, as American statesmen have interpreted all the nation's subsequent wars. The idea became essential to the American national myth.

While the United States was still neutral, Wilson had proposed a "peace without victory," but despite tentative positive responses from the two sides, when Germany resumed a policy of unrestricted submarine warfare in 1917, the president asked Congress (in April) to declare war on Germany. The effect of this decision, certain to tip the military balance, and of the peace proposals Wilson had produced, was to bring the armistice agreement eighteen months later, in November 1918.

Wilson offered a plan for postwar security which would rest upon new international institutions based on American conceptions and values, so as to end what eight decades later Secretary of State Condoleezza Rice, echoing his 1916 rhetoric, would call "the destructive pattern of great power rivalry." Wilson proposed the creation of a League of Nations, that (as he privately acknowledged) would eventually become an American-dominated world government.

A world parliament of sovereign power over existing nations was then, as now, an unrealizable ambition. Even if the American Senate had accepted a commitment to go to war on the vote of the League of Nations (which it refused, the reason it rejected the Versailles Treaty in 1920), neither of America's two main allies, the British and French empires, still intact, would have accepted a League of Nations with the powers Wilson proposed.

Wilson assumed that universal national self-determination would end the destructive role nationalism had played in Europe's past. His views had been formed in ignorance of the actual ethnic, religious, historical, and territorial complexities of the nations and national communities that had been part of the defeated Ottoman and Austro-Hungarian empires. He possessed a very American determination not to be confused by reality or bound by the past (not to be "reality-bound," as a spokesman of another White House, eight decades later, was to say).

He refused to have the history of the Congress of Vienna studied for the lessons it might offer the peacemakers of 1919. He thought good will and a fresh look at the problems by "dispassionate scientists" (an anticipation of Samuel Huntington and the claims of political science), and by Americans distant from the emotions and obscurantisms of Europe, could resolve it all. As early as 1912 he had said to a journalist that he believed God had chosen the United States "to show the way to the nations of the world how they shall walk in the paths of liberty." In practice, the effort to apply the principle of national self-determination left controversial national claims unsatisfied, with large numbers of ethnic nationals on the wrong side of new frontiers (inevitable, without large-scale population transfers), agitating to recover "lost territories."

The Hungarians who found themselves inside Romania, the Sudeten Germans, and the Croats in a newly created Yugoslavia spent the following years resenting the authority of "artificial" new states, contributing to the rise of ethnic hatreds and proto-fascist movements that invited Nazi and Italian Fascist exploitation and hastened the arrival of a second world war—itself touched off by Hitler's claims on the ethnic German borderlands of Czechoslovak Bohemia, and on formerly Prussian territories in interwar Poland. The eventual breakdown of Wilson's First World War settlement was taken in the United States as proof of the incorrigibility of Europeans and as confirmation of the prudence and benefits of national isolation, support for which remained majority opinion in America until 1941. In April 1937 a Gallup poll asked Americans if it had been a mistake for the United States to enter the First World War. Seventy-one percent said "yes." By then there was general agreement that the war had been a tragedy with guilt both on German and Allied sides.[2] This revisionist interpretation of the war said that the United States had been drawn in by its economic stake in an Allied victory and by British propaganda. However, the decision to enter the Second World War was taken out of American hands at Pearl Harbor.

WILSONIANISM ENJOYED A short reprise immediately after the Second World War, which had reopened to Franklin Roosevelt the seeming possibility that had seduced Wilson: that a great armed struggle leading to the "unconditional surrender" of "evil" could secure America's and the world's permanent peace. Shortly after Pearl Harbor, American diplomats were set to work by the Roosevelt administration to draft a new version of the League of Nations. (George F. Kennan would later describe this as a characteristic instance of the American "legalistic-moralistic approach to international problems."[3])

When the Second World War ended in 1945, the spirit of isolationism was still influential in American conservative circles, while at the same time there was a rush of popular sympathy for the suffering of the Russian people and a longing for a renewal of the sense of Allied solidarity that had prevailed during the war. Thus foreign policy was an issue in the 1946 and 1948 American elections. As late as 1949, the leading figure in the Republican Party, Senator Robert A. Taft, objected to American ratification of the NATO treaty, saying that it involved unforeseeable commitments (what would he have made of the idea of NATO in Georgia or Ukraine, or at war in Afghanistan or Pakistan today?). He was, nonetheless, despite himself, a Wilsonian, declaring his support for "international law defining the duties and obligations of nations . . . international courts . . . and joint armed force to enforce the law and the decisions of that court." He felt the new United Nations organization did not yet fulfill these ideals but that it went "a long way in that direction."[4]

He was, despite all, still looking for a way to realize the globally utopian vision of a world parliament that had been Wilson's and Franklin Roosevelt's, which by then had become even for Republicans of isolationist instinct an established belief about how the world of the future should be organized, so that, as Tennyson had prophesied, ". . . the wardrum throbbed no longer, and the battle flags were furled / In the Parliament of Man, the Federation of the World."

The 1948 Communist coup d'état in Czechoslovakia, the

Berlin Blockade, and the outbreak of the Korean War ter-
minated American isolationism, launched the Cold War, and
caused the United States to adopt a policy proposed by a
then-anonymous State Department officer, George F. Kennan.

This policy's intention was "to force upon the Kremlin a
far greater degree of moderation and circumspection than it
has had to observe in recent years, and in this way to promote
tendencies which must eventually find their outlet in either
the break-up or the gradual mellowing of Soviet power." He
saw in this effort a "test of the overall worth of the United
States as a nation among nations ... in which the United
States need only measure up to its own best traditions and
prove itself worthy of preservation as a great nation."[5]

CONTAINMENT'S INCREASING MILITARIZATION during the
1950s, during the Eisenhower administration, reflected the
influence of a more belligerent group of policymakers associated with the international lawyer and militant Protestant
layman John Foster Dulles, descendant of missionaries and
ministers as well as of diplomats, who became Dwight Eisenhower's secretary of state. Historian John Lukacs wrote that
Dulles, a Presbyterian elder and an international lawyer,
"brought with him ... the distressingly puritanical and at
times even pharisaic inclination to see in the world struggle a
national personification of good versus evil, mistakenly ele-
vating the political ideology of anti-Communism into a
superior moral principle." (In 1942, Alexander Cadogan
of the British Foreign Office had described Dulles as "the
woolliest type of useless pontificating American.")

In the presidential campaign of 1952, Dulles called for a "rollback" of Communist power in Central Europe, which unhappily proved hypocritical and mendacious electoral rhetoric and national propaganda, responsible for the deaths of many in the Baltic states who took such American propositions seriously and went into the forests of the region to fight Soviet occupation troops in the mistaken belief that the West would support them. Later, in 1956, Hungarians in rebellion against their Communist government made the same mistake. Despite the revolts in East Germany in 1952, the Hungarian uprising in 1956, and the Polish leadership mutiny that preceded it, nothing was done by Washington to exploit these opportunities to improve the condition of the Central European peoples. At the time of the Hungarian revolt, when Western military intervention was precluded by the risk of general war, Washington refused to consider such political alternatives as an attempt to negotiate a neutralized and disarmed Hungary, or some wider Central European settlement involving mutual troop withdrawals, as the Polish foreign minister had proposed. The events of the Czechoslovakian "Prague Spring" in 1968 offered a new such diplomatic opportunity, which again was ignored.

The notion of a Central European "disengagement" was supported by Winston Churchill before his retirement in 1955, by Field Marshal Montgomery and other British and West European figures, and by Kennan, then at the Institute for Advanced Studies in Princeton. It was rejected in Washington, which had already taken the view that the Cold War had to be fought globally, and that compromise on any front undermined the prospect of "victory" in what

James Burnham (a former Trotskyist, and one of the pro-genitors of the neoconservatives) described in a 1947 book as "the struggle for the world." This American commitment to essentially military conceptions precluded serious West-ern discussion of the possibilities of political action to re-solve the Cold War.

As THE END of the 1950s approached, a colleague, Edmund Stillman, and I circulated an argument that eventually be-came a book, suggesting that the American obsession with Soviet Communist power was turning it toward an Ameri-canized version of Marxist historicism and ideological mes-sianism. We said Washington had fallen under the influence of "the ideological politics of the thirties and moral fervor of the Second World War" in assuming that we and Soviet Rus-sia were now struggling, so to speak, for the world's soul.[6]

We argued that quite the opposite was true. The bipolar Cold War system would pass because Russia was actually backward while Western Europe and Japan were increasingly dynamic. We said that "Europe [is] not dead and [cannot] be expected, either in its western or in its eastern halves, to remain forever in tutelage of America and Russia." We rather floridly declared that "the great introspective and timeless civilizations of Asia" were awakening and would seek power and influence in their turn, contributing to the pluralism of power in international relations. This went against much thinking of the period, which held that the Soviet Union, and the Warsaw Pact countries it controlled, were becoming steadily more powerful, placing the democracies in deadly peril.

We said of Communist internationalism:

> In the early years of the [Soviet] revolution the national element hardly figured; it was the universal messianic dream that counted for most. Lenin had looked West; he believed that "if proletarian revolution were not to break out in Germany, France, England . . . the October Revolution . . . must fail." This did not happen. The result was the Russianization of the ideology . . . coinciding more or less with Stalin's lifetime, the Communist movement became a Russian movement. [By 1960, one was seeing] the beginning of a third phase—the fragmentation of that pan-Russian and imperial dream.

We said that common sense about the nature of Russia's and China's real interests suggested that their theory was false and time was not on their side, so that Kennan's policy of Containment (primarily through political means) of the major Communist powers, allowing the time for what Marx would have called their internal contradictions to undermine them, was the correct one. The interest of China was heterodoxy, to weaken Soviet supremacy among the Communists. Russia itself was in material decline. The United States was mistaken in interpreting Asian nationalism within the rigid limits of its Cold War outlook, as it was doing in Indochina, where it had convinced itself that the

Vietnamese national Communist movement was controlled by China and Russia and posed a serious threat to American global interests, including its military interests. The world in the early 1960s, we said, was already one of developing multipolarity of power and ambitions, in which the United States could flourish but the Soviet Union, in the long term, could not. We ended by recommending patience. Time was working for the United States. The book amounted to an anti-interventionist manifesto, published on the eve of the American commitment to a clandestine war in Laos, and subsequently to military action in Vietnam and Cambodia.

Laos, Vietnam, and Cambodia were the first modern instances of what by now has become an inveterate American policy of direct military intervention in the internal affairs of small non-Western countries when these countries are believed—usually mistakenly—to be victims of some global menace eventually aimed at the United States, so powerful as to render these countries incapable of looking after their own affairs or of forging their own destinies. In such cases the "global" enemy identified in Washington has nearly always proven actually to be nationalism, in the expedient guise of Marxism (in Southeast Asia or Latin America) or instances of radical and xenophobic (that is, nationalistic) Islamic religious radicalism (the case today). The American intervention as a result fails to suppress the supposed enemy, and the United States itself assumes the role of aggressive foreign threat to the national independence of the nation which is the subject of American attention. Defeat is built into such a policy. For incomprehensible reasons this fact seems never to have been understood in official Washington, from the time of the Lyndon Johnson administration to that of the Obama administration.*

THE DULLES ERA of rigid and moralistic foreign policy ideology was followed by the Vietnam crisis, and the Russian-American struggle metastasized, so to speak—at least in American intelligence and policy perception—reappearing on a dozen fronts. What had been a conflict of two nuclear-armed states and rival political systems became seen as a global ideological and moral struggle of epic dimensions, in which the United States had to do political, and if necessary military, battle wherever the symptoms of Marxist thinking could be discerned, from the paddies of Laos to the jungles of Central America.

Dulles had connected the national myth of savior nation with his own fixed notion of bipolar world struggle, a reflection of his religious convictions. This outlook became transformed into a view of Communism—especially of "Asian Communism," mobilizing peasants rather than industrial workers—as a ubiquitous, insatiable, indefatigably resourceful international threat, acting under centralized Communist

---

* I have not included the Kennedy administration in this list because a recent book by Gordon M. Goldstein, the collaborator of the late McGeorge Bundy in the preparation of the memoirs of the latter, who was Kennedy's national security adviser, has published evidence that John F. Kennedy had ordered the withdrawal of all American military personnel from Vietnam by the end of 1965—a step that Bundy himself opposed. Gordon M. Goldstein, *Lessons in Disaster: McGeorge Bundy and the Path to War in Vietnam* (New York: Times Books, 2008).

command. Visiting Saigon in the summer of 1962, I made a note to myself of the U.S. Embassy's political people as "rigid, unimaginative, obsessed with 'Communist timetables for the takeover of Asia.'" China at the time was still generally considered subordinate to Russia, supporting the Vietnamese Communists' insurrection against French colonial power after the Second World War, and then, after 1954, against the American-supported South Vietnamese Republic of Vietnam.

America's Vietnam policy took Marxist (or Maoist) propositions about the development of Communist revolution in Asian societies with extreme seriousness, and held that the Vietnam War had to be won in order to block all of Asia from becoming Communist. (If this were not true, why should the United States bother about what began as a nationalist revolt against France in a distant Asian colony? Americans paid virtually no attention to the anti-French revolt already under way in Algeria in the 1950s, since the Algerian National Liberation Front was not Communist.)[7]

The Dulles vision of bipolar struggle, promoted to global dimensions in the late 1950s, continued to rule American policy thinking until after Communism's collapse. Its influence was still so great in 2001 that George W. Bush automatically constructed his global war on terror as what even at the time could be seen as a parody of the Cold War, even though the enemy in this new version of global struggle was an organization of a few thousand Muslim mujahideen and sympathizers, replacing as enemy in the administration's imagination and propaganda a Soviet Union of 150 million people, possessing the second largest strategic nuclear force on the planet, an imposing economy, and global allies and clients. Astonishingly, this notion was generally accepted in the professional policy community and among the international media. The consequence of this has been the substitution of fictions for fact in important deliberations of government, as repeatedly attested by recent experience. A virtual reality is willed into existence that blocks out reality itself. Sometimes this delusion is driven by domestic political advantage. More often it is a case of personal or collective illusion, motivated by ideology, or private commitments or advantage, that in turn demands confirmation by subordinate officials.

George W. Bush's declaration, following the 9/11 attacks, of a global "war against terror" produced mass alarm among many Americans, who, rather than being fired up with an anger reinforced with confidence, were goaded by morbid and irrational fear into a national mobilization against "terror" characterized by duct-tape-sealed apartments nonsensically stockpiled with survival supplies in Manhattan, Washington, and elsewhere in the country. Official measures ensued, reorganizing bureaucracies, curtailing civil liberties, and reorienting the mission of the all-volunteer army (and its Reserve and the National Guard) that was initially recruited from the American working and lower-middle classes, largely excluded from the profligate prosperity of their governing betters. (This new army's social composition reduced the moderating political influence exercised by the citizen-soldiers and mobilized reserve officers of previous American wars.) In the period following the invasion of Iraq in 2003, the military force was treated in the manner of European colonial armies, increasingly recruited from noncitizens and from candidates for immigration, who were virtually treated as cannon fodder in its rhythm of redeployments and forced—"Stop-Loss"—prolongations of enlistment engagements, resembling military impressment. This treatment was unknown in the citizen armies of the Korean, Vietnam, and world wars. While enlisted "for the duration" in the world wars, American citizen armies, because of egalitarian conscription, were numerous enough that most soldiers did not have to be forced into murderously repetitive deployments.

The Bush "war against terror" was a product of ignorance and political confusion—and probable mendacity, in its claim that the Iraqi despot Saddam Hussein bore part responsibility for the 2001 attacks on New York and Washington. Without evidence, such other Muslim radical groups as the Palestinian Fatah and even the integrist Hamas and Hizbollah—Muslim social revolutionaries, as well as militant movements resisting Israeli occupation of the Palestinian territories—and anti-American and anti-Israeli Middle Eastern groups generally, were held to share in the guilt. From the start, this official and popular conception of America's enemy was extended to radicalism, political extremism, and misrule of many kinds in the non-Western world, all presumed to nourish hatred for the United States because, as President Bush said, "such people hate our freedom."

Pursuing the leadership of al Qaeda and of other radical Muslim groups, and overturning the governments of Afghanistan and Iraq, was not enough. Under neoconservative and Israeli influence at the beginning of 2003, Washington

set about effecting a radical strategic realignment of the entire region. A "Greater Middle East" was to be constructed,
reaching into Central Asia to include Afghanistan as well as
Pakistan, with the invasion of Iraq only the first step. This
policy was unaffected by the subsequent discovery that Saddam Hussein's government possessed no weapons of mass
destruction and had no connection with al Qaeda.

The neoconservative ambition to create a permanent
American alliance with Israel to dominate the Middle East
was already informally a reality but not a success. The
"Defense of the Realm" and "New American Century" initiatives in the two countries rested on the assertion that
Arabs only understand force. It turned out to be the Israelis
and Americans who only understood force, and while the
Arabs ignored (or glorified) their losses, Israel suffered
politico-military defeats without Washington's intervention.
Hizbollah attacks compelled Israel to withdraw from its
twenty-two-year occupation of a "security zone" in southern
Lebanon. Hizbollah gained further influence from its subse-
quent resistance to a second Israeli invasion of Lebanon.
Hamas was strengthened by Ariel Sharon's withdrawal of
Jewish colonies from Gaza. Israel's attack on the Gazans in
2009 produced no advance toward peace with the Arabs.
Israel's moral standing was diminished, particularly in
Western Europe, by the UN-mandated Goldstone Report.
Another new, if not "greater," Middle East was simultane-
ously if inadvertently created by these American and Israeli
measures, which elevated Iran to a position of major Islamic
power in the Middle East, and strengthened Hamas and
Hizbollah. Subsequently, the Obama government's extension

of the Afghan war into Pakistan (and potentially beyond), using drones and special operations forces, has at this writing worsened America's position.

THE COMMON WESTERN assumption about history is that it moves toward an intelligible conclusion, a belief derived from Western religious eschatology. The Enlightenment rejection of religion resulted in an effort to discover autonomous ethical "rules" and a secular pattern in history, leading toward historicist theories, a "belief in . . . speculative systems of history for which there is no objective evidence," which, as the philosopher Karl Popper says, have tended to offer a foundation upon which dangerous political ideologies and movements are built. It is essential to add that they also invite organized violence to make themselves come true.

In the case of the theory, common to liberals as well as many conservatives, of universal progress toward democracy, the presumption made is that the seeming self-evident superiority of democracy makes it the natural end point of history. A foreign policy of military intervention to speed progress toward this inevitable outcome logically follows. Liberalism in its American sense nearly always sees the increasing complexity and interdependence of modern society, and the advance of technology, science, and human knowledge, as evidence of positive change in the moral (and political) nature of humans—an assumption for which there is no evidence. As the philosopher John Gray has written: "No discernable fact or trend has ever supported the belief that

humanity will someday accept one form of government—
Communism, or 'democratic capitalism,' say—as alone legitimate . . . Presupposing as they do a teleological view of
history that cannot be stated in empirical terms, all such theories are religious narratives translated into secular language."[8]

Various systems of historical interpretation ("challenge
and response," "stages of economic development leading to
take-off") or dominant tendencies in man's nature (love of
freedom, material ambition, competitive struggle, power-
seeking, ego, altruism) have been postulated as causing societies to behave as they do. These beliefs are sometimes
influenced by modern systems of economic analysis that
claim scientific objectivity and predictive power, or were
until the great and generally unpredicted financial crisis that
began in 2008 discredited—possibly for good, although that
remains to be seen—certain naive economic dogmas of infallible market efficiency and unvarying rational choice by
economic actors.

A large part of the American foreign policy community
has committed itself to the unproven and unprovable theory that democracy is the "strong" force in history and will
eventually win out over all others. This is convenient, reas-
suring, and highly gratifying to its proponents—or would be,
if it were true.[9] By now, many have discovered that democracy is not the natural (or "default") condition of society,
but is produced in certain political and social circumstances
by values derived from historical experience, and by philosophical reasoning and argument. Or so it has occurred in
modern history. In antiquity, Athens, usually considered to
have been the most perfect example of "direct" democracy,

where citizens gathered at the Agora to make decisions, excluded women and slaves as noncitizens (which presumably would actually make the modern New England Town Meeting the more perfect democracy). Democracy is not created by free elections but by a society's general willingness to accept majority rule, defend minority rights, and accept the nonlethal settlement of political differences. It requires that the powerful submit to civil law and respect the separation of public from private property, freedom of speech, and a free press.

Finally, the ideology of ultimate democratic inevitability ordinarily makes the argument that democracy should be promoted because democracies are innately peaceful. This might seem a common-sense judgment derived from the observation that people do not like conflict and war. It is less easily defended than many think, as the United States fails to disengage from the consequences of its wars "of choice" in Iraq and Afghanistan. If the small wars being indirectly waged in Pakistan, Somalia and elsewhere in East Africa, Yemen, and other countries are included, this makes up a formidable array of wars with states or societies that have done no direct harm to the United States, or for that matter, Israel. The Afghans, Iraqis, Somalis—and Pakistanis and the rest—were supposed to be liberated, not ruined.

IN THE NOT distant past, Hitler, Stalin, and Mao Tse-tung made many destructive decisions because they conformed to ideology and therefore were "objectively" correct, but actually such decisions were the product of what the dictator wished to be true. For example: Stalin's apparent confidence that Hitler would never turn from the Western front to attack Russia, and his consequent failure to prepare for it; Hitler's orders, after Stalingrad, directed to phantom armies; and Mao's ruinous faith in the potential of backyard blast furnaces to manufacture steel.

The American faith that global military struggle with terrorism (identified as Evil), despotism, failed states, and other disorders—with a new and recent emphasis on suppressing addictive drug production and the drug trade—will eventually be solved by American support for democracy is an ideology of self-deception that continues to enjoy the (rather bewildered but seemingly convinced) support of the American public as well as that of the American political class. Since the Second World War, political solutions to foreign policy problems have consistently been sought through military intervention. When the Soviet Union's collapse removed the only external deterrent to U.S. military power, American forces could have been reduced and recalibrated to fit a world of lessened military threat. Instead, the country's military apparatus and the scope of its operations were vastly extended, at the expense of the civilian agencies of American foreign policy, a phenomenon eloquently described by the Washington journalist Dana Priest.*

The process began with the Pentagon's progressive division of the world into "regional commands" under separate American military staffs and headquarters, launching the develop-

* *The Mission*, (New York and London: W. W. Norton, 2004).

ment of an international system of military bases that continues to be extended today to a currently reported total
of some one thousand bases outside the continental United
States. This system now includes major development of
U.S. Pacific Ocean island bases (some disingenuously designated "environmental protected zones") and an effort to
increase the number of bases held and operated in cooperation with allied—or, more accurately, client—countries
in Latin America and in Africa. Each regional command
controls "main operating bases" (MOB) abroad, which in
turn support fully manned "forward operating sites," usually including ground forces and an air base. Beyond them,
"cooperative security locations" are established, not always
permanently manned by Americans but shared with the
forces of allies or clients.

The Vicenza base now being expanded in northern Italy
and the newly built Camp Bondsteel in Kosovo, as well as
bases in Bosnia, Iraq and under construction in Afghanistan
(some the size of small towns), are usually of disputed per-
manence, legal status, and even nomenclature (known as
"enduring" bases in Iraq rather than "permanent" ones).
The acquisition of bases in Iraq (to replace the bases in
Saudi Arabia that the Saudi government forced the United
States to close in 2003 and Iranian bases lost because of the
Iranian revolution in 1979) was an underlying motive for
the American invasion of Iraq. Their future role caused
much difficulty in the "status of forces" negotiations with
the Malaki government in Baghdad in 2008, according to
which American forces promised to make a staged departure of "combat troops" from Iraq.

Under current planning, such bases are to exercise strategic control of the Middle East through their satellite operating sites and "cooperative security locations." The acquisition of seven new joint-use bases in Colombia, bringing half of Latin America into range of U.S. ground-force intervention, was announced in summer 2008, to much controversy and protest elsewhere in the region. The hegemonic implications and intentions of all this, which provides the military structure from which to conduct global interventions or indeed a third world war, are readily acknowledged in Washington and are motivated by what Washington considers internationally valid and progressive reasons.

WHEN THE GEORGE W. Bush administration took office in 2001, one of its announced convictions was that American military forces did not exist to conduct what condescendingly was called "nation-building." The American all-volunteer Army was a war-fighting force. Former Clinton administration secretary of state Madeleine Albright, at the time of the Kosovo war, said that the Eighty-second Airborne Division was not going to be deployed there "to walk little children to school." Nongovernmental organizations, UN peacekeeper forces, or European armies did that sort of thing. The new Bush administration agreed.

Seven years later, during the summer of 2008, as the Bush administration approached its end, Secretary of State Condoleezza Rice conceded that the United States had been wrong. The Bush government now was convinced that nation-building would be the key to success in America's program to bring democracy to Central and South Asia and to the Middle East. She wrote in *Foreign Affairs* that a complete reversal of course on this matter had become essential: "Democratic state-building is now an urgent component of our national interest . . . it is absolutely clear that we will be engaged in nation-building for years to come." She said that this reflected "a uniquely American realism" that taught "it is America's job to change the world, and in its own image." (A uniquely American "realism" had also been cited by the administration in 2003 to justify the invasion of Iraq in order to build democracy there, despite the warnings of many critics in the United States and in what Donald Rumsfeld derisively called "old Europe.")

Secretary Rice continued:

> We have never accepted that we are powerless to change the world. Indeed we have shown that by marrying American power and American values, we could help friends and allies expand the boundaries of what most thought realistic at the time . . . The democratization of Iraq and the democratization of the Middle East [are] linked . . . As Iraq emerges from its difficulties, the impact of its transformation is being felt in the rest of the region . . . Our long-term partnerships with Afghanistan and Iraq, to which we must remain deeply committed, our new relationships with Central Asia, and our long-standing partnerships in the Persian Gulf provide a solid geo-strategic foundation

for the generational work ahead of helping to bring about a better, more democratic, and more prosperous Middle East.*

She then described at considerable length the reconfiguration and retraining that had already begun to prepare the American armed forces, as well as the State Department and other civilian agencies, for the new duties of nation-building that would be theirs over generations to come, in order to "change the world" into one in America's own image.

This had been preceded earlier in the year by reports of reorganization in the diplomatic, development, and aid agencies of government to prepare new coordinated team programs to conduct physical reconstruction, economic development, and civic education in nations that in the future might need rescue from their condition as "failed states," or reclassified from the category of "rogue states," so as to become part of the new world in preparation. There were announcements of prenegotiated contracts with civilian corporations and contractors to prepare nation-building (or rebuilding) plans for nations that might become the objects of American attentions. These attracted little notice at the time, although this program now is operating in Afghanistan, preparing the infrastructure to what during 2009 was expected to become a very large civilian as well as military "nation-building" operation with accompanying military bases there (and possibly in Pakistan, in view of the mounting

---

* "Rethinking the National Interest," *Foreign Affairs* (July–August 2008).

concern of the Obama administration with the supposed need for—or feasibility of—operations there). Few Americans in any case seemed to object to intervention in Middle Eastern, Asian, or African countries to build the foundations for new democratic states, hostile to fanaticism and the rise of terrorist movements, although most have second thoughts when these become wars.

The new American nation-building strategy was presented as an integral part of a program for extending American military and political influence and peaceful development in troubled parts of the world, for which the Pentagon was the lead agency. In congressional testimony in May 2009, Robert M. Gates, Barack Obama's secretary of defense and Republican holdover, confirmed that the new Democratic administration shared this view of the changed mission of America's military forces. A few days later, at a fraught moment in what now was called the Af-Pak war, as Pakistani forces battled the Taliban to recover control of territory north of Islamabad, President Obama declared that America was not relying simply on military force but that he planned a "surge" of civilian development experts and reconstruction specialists into Afghanistan to rebuild the country.

Earlier, in June 2008, before Mr. Obama's election, the Defense Department had issued a new and unscheduled revision of its regularly published statements of National Defense Strategy. A new version of the National Strategy statement, authorized by the Obama government, is said to be in preparation for publication in 2010, although in view of the overall policy continuity between the Bush and Obama administrations it would seem unlikely to greatly differ from its predecessors published in 2005 and revised by Gates in 2008.* The existing 2008 document from Secretary Gates's office provided in its introduction a useful summary of the assumptions of national policy as seen at the time by the military bureaucracy, and of the measures believed necessary to attain the country's objectives.

The salient elements in this introduction were as follows:

> The three principal responsibilities of the American armed forces are to:

> ○ Conduct a global struggle against a violent extremist ideology that seeks to overturn the international system.

> ○ Deal with the threats of rogue-nation quests for nuclear weapons.

> ○ Confront the rising military power of other states.

> These are described as "requiring the orchestration of national and international power over years or decades to come." The National Defense Strategy statement continues with the following specific requirements that American military services are expected to meet:

> ○ Develop long-term innovative approaches to deal with the urgent challenge of al Qaeda's rejection of state sovereignty, violation of borders, and attempts to deny self-determination and human dignity.

* Available on the U.S. Department of Defense Web site, defense.gov.

- Address the inability of many states to police themselves effectively or work with their neighbors to ensure regional security. Armed subnational groups must be dealt with, including but not limited to those inspired by violent extremism, which if left unchecked will threaten the stability and legitimacy of key states and allow instability to spread and threaten regions of interest to the United States, its allies, and its friends.

- Form local partnerships and conceive creative approaches to deny extremists the opportunity to gain footholds in ungoverned, undergoverned, misgoverned, and contested areas affecting local stability and regional stability.

- Counter Iran's pursuit of nuclear technology and enrichment capabilities, and deal with the ability of rogue states such as Iran and North Korea to threaten international order, sponsor terrorism, and disrupt fledgling democracies in Iraq and Afghanistan. Defend South Korea from the North Korean regime's nuclear and missile proliferation, its counterfeiting of U.S. currency, trafficking in narcotics, and brutal treatment of its people.

- Plans must be considered to meet possible challenges from more powerful states that might actively seek to counter the United States in some or all domains of traditional warfare or to gain an advantage in developing capabilities that offset our own, as well as nations that might choose niche areas of military capability and competition in which they might find an operational or strategic advantage, even though some of these competitors may also be diplomatic, commercial, or security partners of the United States.

o In the foreseeable future, while pursuing peacetime engagement between defense establishments, hedge against China's growing military modernization and the effect on international security of China's strategic choices, which are likely to include "anti-access and area denial" assets including development of a full range of long-range strike, space, and information warfare capabilities.

o In the light of Russia's [pre–Georgian crisis] "retreat from openness and democracy" and "bullying of its neighbors" and its more active military stance, resumption of long-range bomber flights, withdrawal from certain arms control and force reduction treaties, and signaled increase in reliance on nuclear weapons for its security, the security implications for the United States, its European partners, and those in other regions must be reassessed as well as the appropriate reaction to Russia's seeming exploration of "renewed influence and seeking a greater international role."

o A mastery of irregular warfare must be achieved to counter measures by prospective adversaries, especially nonstate actors and their state sponsors, to adopt asymmetric methods of warfare and develop or acquire chemical, biological, and especially nuclear weapons. Preparations must be made to deal with worrisome anti-access technology and weaponry that can restrict America's future freedom of action, and also with adversary use of traditional means of influence such as "manipulating global opinion using mass communications venues and exploiting international commitments and legal avenues."

⊚ Strategic measures need to be explored to "secure [meaning to be in a position to control access to] the global commons [space, international waters, aerospace, and cyberspace] and with them access to world markets and resources," using military capabilities and alliances and coalitions, participating in international security and economic institutions, and employing "diplomacy and soft power to shape the behavior of individual states and the international system, and using force when necessary."

The previous *National Defense Strategy Statement*, of March 2005, had stressed the importance of "new legal arrangements to foster greater operational flexibility and rapid deployment," with Status of Forces Agreements demanded from the legal authorities of the states harboring American bases to "protect personnel" and contractors from arrest or prosecution and to "guarantee against transfer to International Criminal Courts."

The striking feature about all these documents is that they say virtually nothing about the physical defense of the

United States. Their whole preoccupation is the defense of American forces present in, or operating in, foreign countries, the prevention of measures by foreign states to "deny" American efforts to intervene in their countries, and foreign states' possible development of measures and technology to resist American intervention.

China and Russia are mentioned in implied terms of possible major hostilities, but otherwise with exclusive attention to the prospect that they might increase their international or regional influence. With respect to major American allies, concern is expressed that they might discover "niche" measures or technologies that might give them an advantage over the United States.

Nuclear weapons proliferation is more than ever an American preoccupation. As in the North Korean case, the most important incentive for obtaining nuclear weapons is to deter the threat of American (or in Iran's case, Israeli) intervention. The only advantage provided by such weapons is defensive: the ability to deter foreign intimidation. As some American policy makers and commentators seem not to have learned from more than sixty years of Cold War nuclear strategy studies, nuclear weapons have no offensive (aggressive or blackmail), or wartime, value unless they are linked to what the strategic studies community describes as a secure second-strike capacity, which is entirely beyond the means of the "rogue" states that preoccupy the United States today.[10]

THE JUXTAPOSITION OF global threat and Wilsonian world reform seems the only way the American national imagination has found to deal with the anxieties and fears produced by the loss of that geographical isolation which for more than a century kept Europe, with its disorders and corrupting influences, and its wars and tragedies, at a seemingly safe distance. The neo-Wilsonianism of the project for extending democratic government to the world is a virtual form of isolationism, a fictional solution to a problem whose previous solution has vanished. Moreover it is a solution in which few of its practitioners truly believe, but for which they lack a plausible alternative.

The United States, as the last-born offspring of the Enlightenment, is the nation perhaps most susceptible to the notion that men and women are all natural democrats waiting to be freed. Thus the administration's apparent conviction at the time of the invasion of Iraq, that once Saddam Hussein and his police and army were defeated, democratic institutions would spontaneously spring up. Similarly, Alan Greenspan expressed astonishment when he found that dismantling Communism in Russia had not "automatically" established a free-market economy.

It is evident that democracy on the American model is not going to be made to prevail in the contemporary world. This leaves the American government and public with an irreconcilable contradiction between the chaotic international realities and stubbornly unsolvable wars they see around them, and the theory on which the government asserts that it acts, and in the service of which it now is engaged in further strengthening its military and foreign political services.

The League of Nations and the United Nations organization, both of them American conceptions, expressions of the American ideology of democratic universalism, were intended to furnish the United States with the security that isolationism had supplied in the nineteenth century. The League, American membership in which was rejected by the Senate, soon succumbed to the forces of totalitarian nationalism in Italy and Germany and of ethnic nationalism in Central and Balkan Europe. The Second World War drew Soviet power, animated by another millenarian ideology, into Central and Eastern Europe and into a place on the UN Security Council—and the Cold War followed.

Two American efforts to reorganize society in order to make the world safe for democracy—which is to say, safe for the United States—had thus failed. The Wilsonian idea, the conviction that the world has to be remade to give the United States security, remained the only solution Washington could imagine to its latest crisis, the challenge of Islamic radicalism. The policy of the George W. Bush administration to make the Islamic states democracies was supported by a neoconservative misreading of history—that after the Second World War the United States had "made" Germany and Japan into democracies. Both of those nations in the past were constitutional monarchies, with parliaments, sophisticated administrative institutions, advanced legal systems and courts, and national political parties. They had little need of instruction in representative institutions, only the motive to reestablish them—which defeat in the Second World War and Allied military occupation amply supplied.

President Bush's second-term inaugural announcement

that America's foreign policy objective thenceforth was "ending tyranny in our world" might cruelly be described as the reductio ad absurdum of the Wilsonian theme in American foreign policy. What eventually will follow is the mystery.

V

America's Elected Enemy

B Y THE YEAR 2000, THE United States had "won" both the
Second World War and the Cold War. The Soviet system and the governments of the satellite states had all collapsed. History, one was assured, had concluded in the
triumph of the liberal-capitalist democratic economic and
political systems. American military bases ringed the world.
American arms faced no challenge. The globalized American economy dominated international investment and finance; the American budget was in surplus.

The United States had no major enemies. It was respected
by most of its former enemies and enjoyed the esteem of
nearly all its past and present allies. One might have thought
the "manifest" destiny Americans envisaged for themselves
had been achieved. But this was not to prove so: External
events, in combination with unsatisfied and unconfessed
national ambitions, meant there was more "history" to
come.

In 1993, the late Professor Samuel P. Huntington of

Harvard University had predicted that the "next" world war—successor to the wars of nations, empires, and ideologies of 1914–1918 and 1939–1990—would be a war between civilizations. He said that what he called an "Islamic-Confucian military connection" was emerging as a challenger to Western civilization, led by the United States.[1] He undoubtedly was writing what he intended as a new paradigm for Washington policy planners, to replace the bipolar Cold War policy paradigm that glasnost and perestroika were rendering irrelevant.

He was mistaken in thinking that some bond would emerge between the Chinese and the Islamic peoples or authorities (at least so far as events have since developed). Arab resentment of the Israeli-American link was already very strong; the Iranian revolution and its seizure of the American embassy, and the Beirut bombings of American and French troops, were relatively fresh memories in 1993. Thinking in conventional Pentagon terms, Huntington proposed a "scenario" in which the Chinese would send advanced weapons to the Middle East for the Arabs to use in fighting the United States.

He offered no clear explanation as to why the Chinese would wish to do this, nor why "the Arabs" would wish to cooperate, in view of the major risks involved and the cultural barriers and incompatibility of interests between Chinese and Arabs, nor did he explain why such a war should be considered a "clash of civilizations." However, as anyone involved in the strategic debates of the late Cold War will recall, China was widely viewed in American policy circles as a potential political or military challenger to the United States (an assumption still widely held). It was believed that China intended to become the "next superpower."

Russia had eliminated itself from this contest and was becoming what it had been before 1917, a core European nation and empire of modest Eurasian scale. Its foreign policy ambitions in the 1990s were to become again one of the concert of international powers and to rebuild a certain regional eminence and security hegemony. China, on the other hand, was considered to be on the geopolitical ascent. It seemed to Huntington plausible to think that China might find arming the Arab states and encouraging them to fight the United States a useful means to its ends.

Huntington failed to anticipate the new dimensions the Middle Eastern conflict would acquire, especially the evolution in contemporary warfare already tending to render conventional high-technology weaponry irrelevant in dealing with highly motivated and popularly supported irregular combatants—the mode of war embraced by Islamic radicals, with explosive international consequences. Writing in the 1990s, he failed to take account of the "lessons of Vietnam." A new and all-professional American army was determined to put Vietnam behind it, so as "by a combination of creative strategies and advanced technologies . . . [to redefine] war on our terms" (as President George W. Bush unwisely said after the fall of Baghdad, in April 2003). This ambition foundered in the low-tech Iraq insurrection, sending the army in 2008 back to "nation-building" among potentially hostile or radical states—a program all but certain eventually to reveal itself (as it had in Indochina) to be equally irrelevant to social and political realities in the non-Western world.

Finally, Huntington would scarcely have imagined that the United States and China would by the 2000–2010 decade have become mutually dependent economies, with the Chinese as mass suppliers to American markets (often as outsourced subsidiaries of American companies) and as financiers of the resulting American consumer trade deficit.

SAMUEL HUNTINGTON MADE the profound conceptual and practical error of treating civilizations, which are cultural phenomena, as if they were nations. Civilizations usually obey no central authority nor have, as such, the political existence of nations. (What city, since Rome, has been the capital of Western civilization?) The United States today is part of Western civilization but does not itself embody it or command it. Western civilization includes all of Western Europe; Europe's satellite societies such as the United States, Canada, New Zealand, and Australia; and all of Latin America, to the extent that the last has been culturally formed by Christian and European ideas and values as well as by its indigenous Amerindian cultures.

China has always been a vast imperial nation with a powerful culture that radiates to the historical kingdoms and cultures on its periphery, but usually it has not directly ruled over the latter but has dominated them by its cultural influence and bureaucratic, military, and commercial power, asking deference from them and accepting their tribute. China also has always possessed an immense complacence, largely indifferent to the world beyond its cultural influence, which, during its history, it has made few attempts to explore—rapidly abandoning even those expeditions and their findings because there seemed to be nothing beyond the oceans to excite China's attention. Its philosophy of existence, or religion if it is to be so called, has been contemplative and introspective, concerned with existence in a universe that is timeless or cyclically reproduces itself, but is not conceived of as progressing toward some purpose or goal (or was not, until the arrival of Western influences and ideas).

Islamic civilization is huge, extending to more than thirty-two countries of majority Muslim population from Africa's Atlantic coast to the Middle and Far East and incorporating most of the northern part of Africa, Zanzibar and Mauritania, part of the Caucasus and much of Central Asia, and including parts of Albania, Bosnia, Bulgaria, and Macedonia in Europe. There are an estimated one and a half billion Muslims in the world, with Indonesia, the fourth most populous country on earth, possessing the largest Muslim population.

Nearly all of the Muslim nations except Iran (and Somalia, which in recent years has mostly lacked government) conduct normal political and economic relations with most if not all of the Western countries. The notion that the members of this global religious civilization are at "war" with Western civilization, or are vulnerable to political radicalization by a few thousand Arab mujahideen because of Middle Eastern and South Asian political issues—of which most of the global Muslim population knows little—is a Western fantasy.

The Western countries are immensely more powerful in

conventional military force than all of the Islamist movements put together, or of all the Muslim armies, even if
those could somehow be mobilized into some grand effort
to overrun the Western democracies. Of the Muslim world's
billion and a half people, fewer than one fifth are Arabs. The
rest are Europeans, Africans, Indonesians (87 percent Muslim), Iranians, Chinese, Turks, Afghans, Indians, Pakistanis,
and other Asians in the Malay peninsula and Southwestern
and Central Asia. Most of these people are ignorant of or indifferent to Arabs, Israelis, and Americans and their allies.
Their national and communal interests are multifarious and
often conflicting, and they have never been under a single
government nor had reason to consider themselves a collective political force in world affairs. They do not add up to
something with which the United States or even Israel could
be "at war."

THIS CONFUSED NOTION that a civilization—an historical,
cultural, and religious entity—goes to war in the way nations go to war was responsible for the willingness of the
American government, press, and public opinion—and international opinion generally—to interpret the attacks in
New York and Washington in September 2001 as the open-
ing acts in a war of Muslim civilization with Western civilization. It was responsible for the Bush administration claim
that America was "going to war" not with a political or sectarian band of zealots but with "terror" or "terrorism," which
the president promised to confront and defeat wherever it

might exist, so as to leave the world cleansed of this "evil" and ready for a global reign of democracy.

As repeatedly has been said, terror and terrorism do not exist as historical entities, only as qualities attaching to human acts. In official discourse and popular opinion terror and terrorism were widely accepted as coded references to a generalized Islamic threat. Even at the time, all this could be seen as incoherent, and the actions and policy explanations of the Bush administration following the September 11 attacks offered little commonsense political and military justification for invasion and war against two Muslim states. The administration and press substitution of the expression "Islamic terrorism" for the unadorned term "terrorism"—a reaction to the radical religious motivations of al Qaeda terrorists—decisively contributed to a seemingly clarifying notion that what really was happening was the fulfillment of Huntington's presumably prescient forecast of a clash of civilizations between the West and Islam.

The reasons for such a war remained unexplained (as they had in Huntington's original formulation of the theory). "Why do they hate us so?" George W. Bush dramatically asked at the time. His answer was that "they [meaning Muslims] hate our freedoms." But Muslims asked the same question after the United States invaded Afghanistan and Iraq. Why this aggressive attack, seemingly on Muslims as a whole, who as nations had done nothing to harm the Western countries? Arabs had fought Turkish and European imperialism. The authors of previous Arab attacks on Western troops in Lebanon, or of the hijackings of Western aircraft or ships, were Palestinian militants fighting Israel, their national enemy, or a handful of politico-religious extremists of whom few Muslims had ever heard. The explanation for the invasion first of Afghanistan and then of Iraq seemed to be that the West now was dominated by Christian "crusaders" who hated all Muslims, and by Zionists.

THERE IS AN authentic clash between Islamic and Western societies, but it is not Huntington's clash of civilizations. Islam and the West are members of, although religious rivals within, the same civilization, that of Mediterranean monotheism.

Islam considers itself to be a prophetic development of the monotheism of Jews and Christians, all of them of Abrahamic descent. Islam is the most recent of them, its prophet, Muhammad, having "completed" the revelation of man's relationship to God that had begun in God's dealings with Adam and subsequently with Abraham and had been further revealed by way of the person Christians believe to be God's incarnate son, Jesus of Nazareth—whom Muslims revere as a prophet.

European civilization, on the other hand, understands itself to be not only Christian but also Greek and Roman in origin and formation. It acknowledges its historical and cultural link to Islamic civilization by way of the tensions and conflicts of religious rivalry, above all in the Crusades, which left lasting impressions on both sides, and in the long Muslim presence in Spain and the Balkans that left those parts of Europe permanently changed.

This essential connection between Western and Islamic history since the time of the Prophet Muhammad (570–632), and his followers' claim to be the inheritors and completers of Jewish and Christian monotheism, is widely unknown, ignored, or misunderstood in the Christian (and Jewish) West, and this ignorance is gravely affecting the events of the twenty-first century.

This is not a trivial point; it is not a quibble over the meaning of the term "civilization." This relationship among the Mediterranean monotheisms has had global influence, in that their interrelated civilization was the dynamic actor in global society until late in the Western Middle Ages, when the essential elements in the growth of the modern world began to emerge in Europe and concurrently Islam entered into what most of its modern thinkers would acknowledge was a decline—a failure to meet the challenge of Western intellectual, cultural, and political development in and after the Renaissance and Enlightenment and in scientific and technological progress.

The issue is important because Islam in the past was at least the match for and in many respects the superior of the West in many secular and scientific realms. Like the other Western monotheisms it is a millenarian religion. It sees existence as progressive and purposeful, leading to a redemptive conclusion of some sort. This is what sets the three apart from most of the other great civilizations—those in Asia, and the lesser civilizations of sub-Saharan Africa and Amerindian Central and South America—which tend to be understood by their members as whole in themselves, not incomplete, not waiting to be "finished" by the return of a

prophet or arrival of a messiah, but fulfilled and meaningful in their own terms. The events, dynasties, and stages of
civilization they have experienced usually are considered
discrete—that is, more or less complete in themselves, suc-
ceeding one another in time but not in meaning, not pro-
ceeding, as in the Western case, from one stage to the next in
a hierarchy of progress and time, nor understood to be directed toward some destined conclusion to which the members more or less consciously aspire and which is expected
eventually to bring peace, or rest, or fulfillment, or perpetual life, or a golden age.

The millenarian nature of the three monotheisms—
meaning that they await a further and promised divine intervention in history, which will put an end to secular time—is
fundamental to the great change in utopian thought and expectation that took place in the West at the time of the Enlightenment. It is essential to an understanding of the era of
modern secular utopias in which we now live.

Among the Western monotheisms, believing Jews still
expect the Messiah's arrival. Muslims await a general judgment followed by heaven or hell. In the Christian (or now
de-Christianized, as many would argue) West, many continue to hold the millenarian expectation of the return of
Jesus the Christ. Since the Enlightenment, dominant intellectual or political forces in what was Christian society have
offered a number of specific theoretical or scientific propositions of human or civilizational progress and fulfillment,
none of which has thus far fulfilled its utopian promise.
Despite the catastrophic experience of the political totali-
tarianisms of the twentieth century, the general expectation

in the West seems to remain that democracy and capitalism, or democratic socialism, will gradually perfect society's institutions, and scientific remedies will be found for human failings.

THE RIVALRY BETWEEN Islam and the European West has existed since the desert Arabs in the seventh Christian century emerged from the Arabian peninsula to confront their neighbors with what they contended were new and final revelations of the monotheistic God. These prophecies provided the doctrinal foundation for a religion preaching and propagating "submission" (the translation of "Islam") to the will of God in the fullness of his revelation in the Qur'an, acceptance of divine judgment, and seeking of salvation. Muhammad's message inspired the prefeudal pastoral and agricultural peoples of Mecca and Medina to overrun and convert neighboring Syria and Iraq and go on successfully to challenge the Christian Byzantines, the Persians, the Egyptians, and the Western Christians. They proposed not only a seemingly progressive religion but a political association that demanded the payment of tribute on the one hand, but on the other hand guaranteed security of persons and property and offered communal autonomy.

The Arabs of the great caliphates that developed in Damascus and Baghdad carried out a phenomenal military and imperial expansion that rapidly reached Kabul, Bukhara, and Samarkand in the east and in the eighth century took the Sind in what now is western Pakistan, took a part of Punjab, and invaded China. They blockaded Byzantine

Constantinople and expanded westward along the southern coast of the Mediterranean. Carthage and eventually Tangier were seized, and peace and an alliance were made with the Berbers. Next was conquest of Spain by a mixed force of Arabs and Berbers, until resistance survived only in the mountains of Asturias. France was invaded, the Pyrenees were crossed, and Narbonne was taken, an expansion halted only at the battle of Poitiers (732–733), which was fought by the Frankish Charles Martel, grandfather of Charlemagne. Charlemagne's counterattack came in 778, but his forces were ambushed in the Pyrenees by the Basques; the event was chronicled in what we know as the *Song of Roland*, in which the knight Roland and the flower of Frankish chivalry perished. (This was five hundred years before the Crusades.)

The astonishing political and military achievement of the Arabs in so rapidly establishing an empire extending from the Atlantic to Central Asia incorporated many separate peoples, including Christians and Jews, and adapted and made use of the intellectual and scientific achievements of Greek civilization, translated into Arabic. The version that emerged in Andalusia of this distinctive Muslim civilization was undoubtedly the most imposing achievement of the early Middle Ages, without counterpart among the more backward Christian Europeans until the time of the Renaissance, to which the Arab revival of classical civilization contributed. The American historian David Levering Lewis writes:

> Muslim Europe and Christian Europe faced each other in a delicate equipoise at the great Pyrenees

divide. Andalusia's golden age unfolded in the reign of the remarkable amir and [Umayyad dynasty] caliph 'Abd al-Rahman III. His palace city on the slopes of the Sierra de Córdoba, three miles northwest of the Andalusian capital, was an architectural hyperbole whose remains beggar Versailles as, in the caliph's time, its colonnaded great halls, geometric gardens, and cascading fountains humbled generations of ambassadors and awed subjects . . . Córdoba's seventy-odd libraries amaze modern scholars as much as they stunned literate Christians of the late tenth century. There would be nothing at all comparable elsewhere in the West to the city's main library of 400,000 volumes.[2]

In Muslim Andalusia, as later in the Muslim-controlled Balkans, Christians and Christianity were tolerated, merely taxed. Jews were treated well.* The empire the Arabs created, and that the Ottoman Turks eventually inherited (without Moorish Spain, the reconquering of which was completed by

---

*   This was generally true in the Arab and subsequent Ottoman empires, where non-Muslims were allowed to live peacefully in communities under their own leaders, so long as they conformed to the political and social order, paid their taxes, et cetera. Christians served in the Ottoman army both as conscripts (the Janissaries, who became an important political force when the empire fell into decline) and as volunteers. Christian Armenians had a large commercial role in the Ottoman Empire, as did Christian Greeks, and many Greek families held important appointments in the imperial administration. This tolerance did not prevent discriminatory fiscal measures with respect to the non-Muslim communities, as well as occasional outbreaks of sectarian violence.

the taking of Grenada by Ferdinand of Aragon and Isabella of Castile in 1492), lasted eleven centuries. The authority of the Sublime Porte finally collapsed as a consequence of Ottoman defeats in the Balkan Wars and the First World War, when Turkey was imperial Germany's ally.

THIS REMARKABLE ACHIEVEMENT remains a crippling legacy to Islamic society today. No possibility has seemed evident by which modern Arabs might emulate and reproduce these accomplishments of their past. The relative decline of Islamic society began in the late Middle Ages as the West European nations' global explorations and conquests were launched, providing geographical and technological knowledge and advantages and advancing their development of social and political institutions, while Muslim society remained essentially feudal in organization.

Because of Qur'anic teaching, Islam had difficulty in separating political from religious power, or philosophy from theology,* as the Christians did from very early in the history of church and state. This was vital to the West's eventual development of independent scientific and political thought. The dual structure in Christian society, with religious authority proper to the pope, vicar of Christ on earth, and the emperor as inheritor of the autonomous political and secular authority of Caesar, had its basis in the teaching of Christ in the New Testament concerning the things of God and the things

---

* Philosophy is defined here as the use of natural reason to reach autonomous conclusions about the ultimate nature and causes of things; theology as the application of reason to divine revelation.

of Caesar. The emperor ruled a political order, derived from the Roman system in which Christianity had begun, in possession of generally acknowledged legitimate and autonomous political power. He deferred to papal authority in religious matters, but only in that. Governing was a matter for the lay orders or estates of society, including the emperor or king, who was invested with the "divine rights" of monarchy acknowledged by the Church. Even though the Catholic Church maintained into the 1960s a position of theoretical condemnation of democracy, on grounds that morality cannot be subjected to majority vote, at the Second Vatican Council in 1965 it abandoned that position in its Declaration on Religious Freedom. It did so on the revisionist philosophical grounds argued by the American Jesuit John Courtney Murray: that the free exercise of individual conscience is a supreme value.

Islamic political society today generally remains confined within a religious dogma that is considered immutable, as presented in the original Arabic text of the Qur'an, the canonical version of which was determined in the seventh century (651–652).* The long-term consequences have been

---

* Muslim students ordinarily learn the Qur'an by rote in a classical Arabic few actually speak or understand. The book itself is not considered a record or text but the living word of God, God's Presence on earth, in some sense analogous to the consecrated communion Host of Catholicism. This is why the Qur'an's abuse or desecration by American soldiers and interrogators in the Iraq war seemed to Muslims to validate the widespread conviction that Americans were not merely enemies of Islam but depraved. See Michael Peppard, "The Secret Weapon, Religious Abuse in the 'War on Terror'" in *Commonweal* (December 5, 2008).

lasting economic and scientific backwardness, as documented by Muslim scholars and intellectuals in the Arab Human Development Report issued in 1999 under the auspices of the United Nations Development Program. Its uncompromising analysis of the backwardness of education and thought in the Muslim world noted the historical emphasis on authority in Muslim life and education and a traditional fear of "chaos" and schism that tends to induce hostility to innovation and intellectual questioning. A Syrian intellectual is quoted as saying that "the role of thought has been to explain and transmit . . . not to search and question." Theology has been limited to elucidation rather than analysis and extrapolation.

THE LONG TRADITION of collective Muslim political existence, begun with the great Arab caliphates in Damascus, Baghdad, then in Spain, culminated in the Ottoman Empire, which at its fullest extent in the early nineteenth century was the largest of all existing state systems, without really being a state or modern at all. It was ruled by a family, the House of Osman, by no rigid code but through a grand vizier named by the family and given absolute powers. He acted through secretaries and local councils in a manner closer to empires of antiquity than to nineteenth-century Europe, being in many ways flexible and tolerant, not asking ideological conformity, religious conversion, or social confirmation but only obedience, tribute, and taxes. The system was open to the ascension of talent among the conquered, and social status, even of slaves, was no necessary obstacle to success; members of the governing imperial household were "slaves" of the sultan and many, the descendants of conquered peoples, actually were slaves.

It was a system that could not survive, although until late in the nineteenth century it was more successful than the Hapsburg empire in dominating its "internal nations." The Young Turk movement, begun mainly by exiles in Europe, was responsible for a revolution in 1908 that forced the sultan to restore the constitution and hold elections and was meant to reconstitute the empire on a liberal and national basis. It contributed instead to dissension among nationalities and to unrest in the army. Meant to reform the system as a whole, it actually proved a step toward its disintegration. In 1916, the Hashemite Grand Sharif of Mecca, Hussein, proclaimed himself king of the Arabs and launched the successful Arab Revolt against the Turks (with the British officer T. E. Lawrence—"of Arabia"—as a military advisor to Hussein's son Faisal, who commanded the irregular Arab army, which functioned in cooperation with British forces taking orders from Cairo).

At the end of the Great War, the military hero Mustapha Kemal Pasha (later called Kemal Atatürk) refused to accept the empire's dismemberment, as imposed by the Allies' Treaty of Sèvres in August 1920, and led Turkish troops in expelling the American, French, and Italian occupation forces in Turkey and in defeating a subsequent Greek intervention. His creation of the homogeneous and secular modern Turkish nation-state was to have no parallel elsewhere in the post-imperial Islamic world.

The legal scholar Noah Feldman notes that premodern

Islamic societies were mostly governed by a division of authority between military officers, sometimes non-Arabs, and religiously trained legal scholars, and he says this informal compact, comparable to, but different from, feudal arrangements in the West, conferred legitimacy on the rulers on condition that they upheld the authority of the scholars. The system encouraged "stability, executive restraint, and legitimacy." Through their near monopoly on legal affairs in a state where God's law was accepted as paramount, the scholars built themselves into a powerful and effective check on the ruler. To see the Islamic constitution as containing the balance of powers so necessary for a functioning, sustainable legal state is to emphasize not why it failed, as all forms of government eventually must, but why it succeeded so spectacularly for as long as it did.[3]

Exactly because the Ottomans in the nineteenth century felt the need to modernize their system, they made a series of administrative reforms which brought legal administration under direct state control. Malise Ruthven writes that "[t]he single most durable feature of the reforms turned out to be the removal of effective lawmaking authority from the scholars through the substitution of written legal codes for the common law of the Shari'a."[4] By the elimination of their interpretative function with respect to God's law, the scholars were deprived of their political influence, leaving the sultans, effectively, with absolute power. This, according to Feldman, then became the dominant political model for Sunni Muslims in the twentieth and twenty-first centuries.

In what also had been meant by the Ottoman authorities

to be a modernizing consolidation of public services under state administration, the institution of the *waqf* lost influence. The undermining of this independent trust or foundation which from medieval times had fostered public welfare through nonstate hospitals, schools, mosques, inns, and other public services and functions would, in turn, weaken what today might be called the mediating and accountable institutional "civil society" of the Muslim state, to the advantage of state power, although the institution of the *waqf* survives.

Hence as the Ottoman state approached its end, the Young Turk reforms failed. The scandal and success of Atatürk was to make the revolutionary decision to establish a secular republic and abolish the caliphate in 1924, thus disestablishing Islam as state religion, breaking clerical power, forbidding distinctive religious garb (the veil and the fez), and making the army custodian of the lay state.*

The questions of intellectual, social, and political modernization that Atatürk answered, if only partially, confront all the Islamic societies today. His secular state was presumably meant to leave religion behind, no doubt to wane away as, in his time, Christianity seemed to be doing in Western Europe. Quite the opposite has happened, in Islam as well as in Turkey itself, which nonetheless remains a secular and democratic state, the only one in the Islamic Near and

---

* The Turkish army has exercised this responsibility in recent years by overturning governments under clerical influence in 1960, 1980, and most recently in 1997; however, a reformed version of the pro-Islamist party forced from office that year was reelected in 2002 and governs today.

Middle East, allowing exception for multiconfessional Lebanon, which is balanced precariously among predatory powers.

Since the First World War, there has been little of that progress toward democracy that should have occurred elsewhere in the Islamic Middle East under the American ideology of democratic inevitability. The ambition of the Arab elites was modernization. It was also the ambition of the European mandatory powers that under the League of Nations system took effective power in the eastern Mediterranean in 1920. Later, after the Second World War, the residue of imperialism, the Cold War, and the Arab-Israeli wars contributed further to crippling that ambition. Yet it is the Muslim and Jewish peoples of the region who, for better or worse, must be held responsible for what has happened to them and will happen. In the absence of secular political reform, many Muslims now are turning to a recognizably utopian, and ultimately futile, form of revolt—that of the Islamists.

RESISTANCE TO FOREIGN intrusion and occupation is a primordial impulse in any society anywhere. It is a matter of defending communal integrity and identity. This ultimately lies behind the hostility toward the United States and the West that widely exists in the non-Western world. They are seen as propagating what seems a sterile and aggressive culture. The other ways by which men have organized their existence and sensibility have been shattered in the past three hundred years by the impact of Western science, industrialism, and imperial ambition. The consequence is a Westernization of international society that until recently was presented in the benign guise of an enriching, progressive, and above all inevitable "globalization," but has today assumed to many a cruel and destructive character.

Islamic civilization has been the greatest victim of this development. The shock cannot be underestimated. The Islamic reaction has fostered a present-day miasma of theories created elsewhere about an alleged inborn Islamic disposition to violence or terrorism (promoted by Western intellectuals who should know better, Huntington himself among them). The "war on terror" has fostered the use in serious matters of the vulgarized residue of such ideas, as in Bush administration and neoconservative rhetoric about "Islamo-Fascism." It underlies the intellectually disreputable practice of some Western polemicists of casting political affairs in metaphysical language (e.g., "axis of evil") that implicitly characterizes Muslim enemies as Satanic, which even among nonreligious Western audiences evokes a certain cultural atavism. This has tended to discourage (or in the America national case, even render "un-American") dispassionate treatment of the actual, interest-based, and rational motivations and intentions of Islamic societies and states, thus thickening the fog of ignorance and malice within which Western government decisions have often been taken. The West's political, military, economic, and cultural expansion, and the efforts of other societies to reject it, deal with it, or accommodate to it, have provided one of the underlying narratives essential to the understanding of contemporary events.

The instinctive and direct response to Western intrusion has always been resistance, often armed resistance, as in the cases of the Indian army mutiny (the "Great Rebellion") in 1857 and the rise of the Mahdiyya movement in the Sudan at roughly the same time, the one against colonial practices and the second against imperial conquest. The Sudanese fundamentalist government that came to power in 1986 and harbored al Qaeda in the 1990s, Feldman writes, "was led by the ideological descendants of the Mahdists [who ruled Sudan exactly a century earlier]." The Dervish armies of the "Messenger of Allah" and his successor stopped the East African advance of the British Empire for the better part of a decade, after the Mahdi Mohammad Ahmed had seized Khartoum in 1885 and massacred the British garrison (including General Charles ["Chinese"] Gordon, hero of the earlier T'ai P'eng [Taiping] Rebellion).* The "nationalist" inspiration and the fundamentalist religious motivations of the two movements, the Muslim and the Chinese, closely resembled one another.[5]

A second form of reaction has been a loss of confidence in or rejection by the victim society of its own seemingly discredited local culture, with radical conversions to foreign values and techniques, as in the case of the Chinese "New Tide" movement at the National University in Peking, beginning in 1917. Its leader demanded adoption "of the new Western method in all things . . . not [confusing] the issue

---

* Dervishes were members of Muslim religious (and military) orders who had taken vows of poverty and lived as mendicants, like Christian friars.

by such nonsense as 'national heritage' or 'special circumstances.'"[6] This obviously anticipated the Chinese Communist cultural capitulation to modernity, whose leaders made use of Marxism-Leninism, a "progressive" Western millenarian and revolutionary ideology that promised to be able to transport society into a new age, far in advance of not only the established and seemingly reactionary kingdoms and cultures of Asia but of the bourgeois capitalism and imperialism of the existing West as well. Thus the Chinese, Vietnamese, and other modern Asian Communist movements were inspired to believe they could, so to speak, leap over the imperialist and capitalist stages of Marx's historical and revolutionary scheme to arrive in a postmodern future through adoption of Marxist-Leninist doctrine and organizing Communist societies. This failed dramatically.

A third, and in the end inevitable, form of response has been the attempt to make a creative synthesis of the challenging foreign intrusions with existing norms and values. This is obviously the most logical (and historically necessary) response, and the most frequent, but it is not always the most successful. It usually has amounted to a form of abdication, although seeming otherwise, as the failures of the non-Western world demonstrate—from the commonplace hereditary dictatorships of the non-West today, through mafia capitalism, to the nations bribed into undergoing stripmining of their national resources while their duly elected presidents possess châteaux in the Loire Valley or stately homes in England.

Finally there is the phenomenon that may be described as "magical irrealism," which was most common in Africa in the colonial period, in the form of nativist cults appropriating symbols and doctrinal fragments from Western missionaries in the effort to "steal" the apparent magic that had given the foreigners their superior power. In its original form it still is not uncommon in Central Africa, and at its most sophisticated it could be seen in the Khmer Rouge movement in modern Cambodia, which took power in 1975 from an American-backed military regime after prolonged American bombing and invasions by Americans and both South and North Vietnamese forces had left the country in ruins.*

The ambition of the Khmer Rouge was to rescue or to recreate a progressive version of Khmer civilization by forcing the people out of the cities and back onto the land, killing all the Western-educated Cambodians and eventually all those they could find who were educated at all; evacuating factories, closing schools, murdering professionals and "intellectuals": in fact finally killing a tenth of the population. The successful Communist Vietnamese government in Hanoi eventually invaded Cambodia in 1978 to block the Khmer Rouge's mad attempt to save Cambodia's people by destroying modernity itself. (Hanoi's intervention took place against American government objections; U.S. official hostility to the Vietnamese Communists remained stronger than resistance to a genocide provoked by past American policies.)[7]

This was roughly the same period as the political hysteria of the Cultural Revolution and Red Guards movements in

---

* The past scope and character of non-Western responses to the imperialist and colonialist West is discussed at length in Stillman and Pfaff, *The Politics of Hysteria: The Sources of Twentieth-Century Conflict* (New York and London: Harper & Row and Victor Gollancz, 1964).

Maoist China, which were equally set on rejecting the culture of the Chinese past, destroying its schools and educated class and creating a fantasy version of modernism, with industry composed of backyard steel smelters and peasant factories.

IN THE ISLAMIC world, the violent defense of cultural identity and religion has taken place primarily in the Middle East and Central Asia, where the modern confrontation with the Western powers, and in recent years with the United States in particular, has been most intense and disruptive. It is customary in sympathetic Western circles, as well as in Islamic countries themselves, to blame modern Islam's political crisis on Western imperialism and colonialism and to ignore the responsibility of Muslims themselves and of Islam as a religion for the obstacles to development that characterize the Muslim world's current plight, but the matter is more complex.

The crisis has been intensified politically by post-war geopolitical pressures and the Western pursuit of access to Middle Eastern energy resources, as well as by the destructive effect economic globalization has had on traditional subsistence, agricultural, and trading economies. The globalization of international communications and media, as well as of popular culture (mainly in the form, initially, of strictly censored international television and luxury consumer advertising to elite audiences, but recently turning into virtual saturation by satellite television, much of it Western, but increasingly of Arab origin), and the eruption in 2008 of Western capitalism's own internal crisis, devastating to much ambitious development intended to create self-sufficient economies, have further contributed to the social and economic aspects of Islamic society's problems. The privileged in Arab societies have tended to readily adapt themselves, at least superficially, to the Western world, essentially on the West's own terms and usually at a cost to Islamic orthodoxy. The wealth of raw materials held by the energy-producing Muslim countries has led to flamboyant modernization in some parts of the region, but frequently without installing social and economic development that could survive the windfall from minerals, oil, and gas and benefit the entire society.*

This superficial modernization, accompanied by a narrow liberalization among the privileged classes, has failed to make a serious difference to the basic problems presented by the Islamic religious and moral inheritance. The most powerful fundamentalist movement remains that of Wahhabi Saudi Arabia. The country is the main financier of integrist and fundamentalist schools and mosques in the region that teach according to the strict norms of Wahhabi doctrine. For nearly a century Washington has supported the Saudi government and, indirectly, Wahhabi fundamentalism, against such secular reform movements as Egyptian president Gamal Abdel Nasser's 1950s "Arab Socialism"

---

* Ali A. Allawi, a former Iraqi minister, writes in *The Crisis of Islamic Civilization* (New Haven: Yale University Press, 2009) that while Saudi Arabia has "demolished 95 per cent of historical buildings in the sacred cities of Mecca and Medina," the Gulf city-states are characterized by "rampant commercialism, brand worship, gigantism, strict class segregation and a calendar of 'festivals' and 'events' designed by marketers." Quoted in *Prospect* (London), September 2009.

and the originally modernizing and secular Ba'ath movement in Iraq and Syria. The secular reform parties were
seen (no doubt correctly) as threatening American oil interests in the region and as actually or potentially sympathetic
to Washington's Cold War enemy, the Soviet Union, sup-
porter of radical liberation movements inside and beyond
the Middle East.

Islamic societies elsewhere, and the Muslim diaspora in
Europe, have been affected by these developments, but the
center of the intellectual—and theological—crisis remains
the Middle East, where in modern times there have been
several Islamic reform initiatives, some progressive, but most
promoting return to strict interpretation of the Qur'an and
to scrupulous observance of its teachings. The origins of fundamentalist reform are best known in the West because of
the success of the Wahhabis, and by the more recent appearance of other versions of fundamentalism hostile to the
Saudi monarchy.

ISLAMIC "INTEGRISM," AS the term implies, calls on believers to make the Islamic religion "integral" to their lives.
Fundamentalism is a mode of literal doctrinal or scriptural
interpretation, just as it is in Christianity and Judaism. The
militancy of both expresses the deep force of religious "nationalism" in Islamic societies, understanding nationalism
in its widest sense as the impulse to defend a certain conception of collective identity as expressed in religion, culture, and political life—as in the case of the Taliban, to take
the most visible current example.

Hence the Western attempt to deal with this hostility through military intervention, control, and "nation-building," as the United States (and NATO) are currently attempting to do, is a misconceived effort, all but certain to fail, whatever the superficial and transient successes. The intervention will fail because it offers only the illusion of relevant reform, while itself conveying still more of the disruptive force of Westernizing modernity, political change, and cultural and economic globalization. This has tragic or at best demoralizing consequences for the present-day Muslim societies that are the objects of American and NATO attention. It is not unlikely that the consequences for the invading countries may prove tragic as well, as a result of the hubris of an attempt to deliver a form of Western values at gunpoint.

Contemporary fundamentalists are usually identified with the nineteenth- and early-twentieth-century revivalist movement called Salafism, a reference to the first generation of Muslims (*salaf* means "ancestors" or "founders"). The Salafists held that the West had appropriated important Muslim principles, while Islam itself had grown weak. These ideas influenced the Muslim Brotherhood, which was founded in Egypt in 1928, and as Wendy Kristianasen has written in a summary of its influence, it "rapidly grew into a vast, popular, social and political movement with hundreds of thousands of members across the Arab world."[8] It was anticolonial (and later, pro-Palestinian) and some of its members were to fight in the 1948 war to defeat the Zionists in partitioned Palestine. The Palestinian Islamic Jihad and Hamas descend from the Brotherhood, whose members remain the principal political opposition in Jordan and Egypt. The Brother-

hood was banned for a time in Egypt, indeed "nearly anni-
hilated," because it had opposed Gamal Abdel Nasser's military coup d'état in 1952.[9]

Nasser's successor, Anwar el-Sadat, allowed it to reemerge,
and after he was assassinated by radical Islamists in 1981
the Brotherhood renounced violence and declared its support for parliamentary government. It is today allowed to
run electoral candidates in Egypt as independents, and it is
estimated to have 2.5 million members and a much larger
number of sympathizers there, but has done poorly in elections. The government calls it an "extremist" movement
and exaggerates its current importance in order to encour-
age Washington's tolerance of the absence of real democratic reform in Egypt. Egypt is a religiously heterodox
country mixing Sunni and Shia traditions, with one third of
its male Muslims also members of Sufi orders (and twice that
number who celebrate Sufi festivals), plus Nubians, many
Coptic Christians (10 percent of the total population) and
anti-Muslim Bedouins, and secular nonbelievers.

President Nasser was responsible for hanging the man
considered the most important intellectual and moral influence on modern Islamic radicalism, Sayyid Qutb, born in
1906. He traveled in the United States in the late 1940s and
admired Western literature (especially the English Romantics) while rejecting Western society as dehumanized and
dehumanizing. He found abhorrent the idea that Islam
could or should borrow from Western thought or from Enlightenment ideas. He concluded that modern Arab society
had fallen into a near-pagan state of *jahiliya*—of ignorance
and the effective apostasy of leaders that would justify

violence, just as Muhammad had found it necessary to fight the Meccan pagans before they would submit to Islam. He was imprisoned and executed in 1966 by Gamal Abdel Nasser's police, but his prison writings provided the rationale for the assassination of President Sadat in 1981 and for subsequent Islamist attacks on government officials, Westerners, and tourists in Egypt.

Qutb had been influential during and after the Second World War in introducing Nazi themes into Islamic Judeophobia, as well as simultaneously providing a note of Western philosophical "authenticity" to modern Muslim thought by encouraging resistance to social injustice, the deification of man, and religious prejudice. (His criticism of Jews was for the power they allegedly possessed and abused, not for their religious beliefs.) Malise Ruthven wrote in 2008 that Qutb's version of Islam, like that of some others who had studied in the West and returned disillusioned, was untraditional, to an extent invented. Ruthven added that in modern fundamentalist religious movements in Christianity and Judaism as well as in Islam, the attraction has tended to be to people educated in the applied sciences and technology, such as engineering and computer programming, where the subject matter is fixed and unsusceptible to critical thinking, a matter of certitudes. This was the case for several of the 9/11 bombers, and for others involved in Muslim terrorist episodes.

THE NOTION OF reestablishing the caliphate was not part of the original fundamentalist movement or al Qaeda political ideology but seems to have been the invention in 1952 of a

Palestinian jurist, Taqiuddin Nabahani, who had studied at al-Azhar University and was a member of the Muslim Brotherhood. He broke with the Brotherhood in publishing a book in 1950 in which he argued that the most serious obstacle to the Palestinians' recovery of their country from Israel was Palestinian nationalism, which copied the concepts and techniques of the original Asian and North African "national" liberation movements. So long as the Palestinian "nation" was pitted against Israel it would lose, Nabahani argued. As a nation it did not exist.

His argument was parallel to the call for reconstitution of the "Arab Nation" that had been influential between the world wars and in the 1950s. He said an Arab federation had to be established like that which had existed from the time of Muhammad until Baghdad fell to the Mongols in 1258. This seemed a more effective vehicle for resistance to the West, offering a vision of the reunion of millions of Arabs who until recently—the defeat of the Ottoman Empire had occurred just some three decades before—had thought of themselves as members of a single social and political entity distinguished by religion.

Taqiuddin Nabahani formed a political party called Hizb ut-Tahrir, which ran candidates in several elections in Jordan, but by the end of the 1950s he decided that his program could not succeed through electoral methods and resolved to create an underground movement based on individual cells. This attracted the attention of intelligence services across the region, and by the 1970s, Nabahani having been killed, the movement seemed to have been completely suppressed.

Twenty years later the group reappeared in Central Asia, notably in Tajikistan and Uzbekistan, where the people of the ex-Soviet Muslim republics wanted to reclaim their Muslim identity, as did some members of the Asian Muslim immigration in Western Europe, particularly in Britain. The group also found adherents in Indonesia. It publishes two quarterly journals in Britain, from where its ideas have been exported to the Indian subcontinent. The group's activities are considered legal in Britain, but it has had problems there and in Denmark and Germany because of its hostility to Israel. In France and Spain its cells are illegal.

According to an analysis in June 2008 by Jean-Pierre Filiu in *Le Monde diplomatique,* "As a transnational phenomenon Hizb ut-Tahrir is at home in a globalized world and this ease may explain its return to popularity. It also shows how such marginal or extremist networks compensate for their weakness through projecting their desires onto an abstract fantasy of Islamic unity. In October 2006 al Qaeda, denying the reality of its marginal status, proclaimed the foundation of a virtual caliphate and entrusted the task of setting up as an Internet presence to a jihadist in Baghdad." According to Filiu, "the result was pathetic."[10]

The idea of a revived caliphate has nonetheless attracted much attention in Washington, despite its utter lack of political feasibility, and President George W. Bush solemnly described it (in September 2006) as posing the threat of "a totalitarian Islamic empire encompassing all current and former Muslim lands, stretching from Europe to North Africa, the Middle East and Southeast Asia." (No real caliphate ever reached from Europe to Southeast Asia.)* The Heritage Foundation and the Nixon Center have sponsored studies and seminars on Hizb ut-Tahrir (which calls itself "HT" in the English-speaking countries), in which some have attributed to it (without hard evidence) a million activists in forty countries, calling it a "new Comintern."

The idea also serves for both Islamists and their American enemies as a remarkably guileless paradigm for the entire Islamic "war" against the West, which for more than eight years has been essentially a fantasy in which, aside from a few sensational bombings in Western Europe, of often uncertain provenance, the United States and its allies have participated more eagerly than the Muslims themselves.

Al Qaeda's illusion that the Grand Caliphate might be restored seems shared by so weighty a figure as Henry Kissinger, who has expressed concern that "a universal political organization" based on a fundamentalist interpretation of the Qur'an would leave "little room . . . for Western notions of negotiations or of equilibrium in a region of vital interest to the security and well-being of the industrial states."[11] This

---

* Much of the movement's success among Muslim students is due to the fact that membership is free of obvious cost. The movement rejects any form of armed action, and in Israel and Palestine it refuses to participate in elections. Hence membership runs no risk of reprisal from either Israel or the Palestinian authorities—or even of an election failure. As Filiu says, in his 2008 article, HT's popularity is due to its "refusal to engage in concrete politics and [to] an extraordinary accumulation of despair [on the part of young Muslims at the seeming impotence of their society]." The movement provides a fantasy that compensates for the failure of Palestinian and Arab resistance to Israel and the United States.

view of balance as the objective of diplomacy contrasts fundamentally with that of former Republican secretary of state Condoleezza Rice, repeatedly expressed, that the Westphalia system of balance of power is outmoded, "leads only to war," and should in the interests of all be abolished and replaced with an association of democracies led by the United States—a view that seems shared by figures in the Obama administration.[12]

There is a persistent belief among American analysts and politicians that today's manifestations of fundamentalist Islamist violence are of unprecedented character and scope. John McCain was asked in 2008 by *Fortune* magazine what the greatest threat to the U.S. economy is, and he replied, "Well, I would think that the absolute gravest threat is the struggle we're in against radical Islamic terrorism, which can affect, if they prevail, our very existence."[13] A similar belief is commonly heard in journalistic discussion, but it also exists in the academy, where Columbia University professor Philip Bobbitt said in a 2008 book, which gained serious attention, that Islamic insurgence could combine with modern nonstate organizational and communications possibilities to threaten modern society itself. The British historian Niall Ferguson called Bobbitt's the most important political work written since the Second World War.[14]

Yet the notion of a new "universal" caliphate incorporating any of the advanced industrial societies of the present-day West is surely to any realistic observer a delusion. The Western states are immensely more powerful by any measure. The fundamentalist movement is internally divided and materially weak. For reasons of cultural solidarity Islam may be mobilized to resist foreign aggression or invasion, but overall it falls into that category of political societies that can be described as invulnerable to invasion but incapable of successful aggression. As in the case of China or Russia, the invader is simply swallowed up and finds himself digested or assimilated, without ever effectively controlling what he has conquered; and eventually he is spat out.

This, one would think, will be the unfortunate fate of Barack Obama's attempted military solution to the crisis by shifting the weight of the American war in the Muslim world from Iraq to the Afghanistan-Pakistan front, sending a "surge" of military reinforcements to Afghanistan—expected to bring the total to more than 100,000 by the spring of 2010—and sending just as large a surge of American civilian development specialists, auxiliaries, contract workers, and "security" mercenaries. Few of these can be expected to have an appreciation of what really will be entailed in any American effort to take effective control (with the principled rationale of building a democracy there—and in Pakistan), nor why the forty million Pashtuns in the region, as well as the separatists of Pakistan's Balochistan Province, and neighboring India, Kashmir, Tajikistan, Uzbekistan, Turkmenistan, Iran, and even Yemen, will not all prove actively hostile to such an undertaking.

ELSEWHERE THAN IN Iraq and Afghanistan-Pakistan, al Qaeda's existence remains largely notional. Its real objective (and the base for its association with the Taliban) is destruction of the Saudi monarchy, which sponsors the rival

Wahhabi interpretation of strict Islamic observance. The phenomenon is essentially an affair of intra-Muslim doctrinal and political rivalry in which Westerners are secondary players (unwelcome, and ultimately dispensable).

A dispute exists among specialists as to whether al Qaeda, as such, is really a structured and disciplined international movement with a leadership and staff in Waziristan, or whether it is a mutually supportive international association of self-nominated enthusiasts and groups with local as well as international grievances. There is a question whether in the West it is—as some Western police specialists have suggested—mainly a phenomenon of "guys hanging out," motivated by a thirst for glory and adventure and influenced by what they hear at the mosque or have read in the papers about the war in Iraq and the bombing of Afghanistan and Pakistan. Some possibly have "trained" in Waziristan, but as it takes very little training to acquire the knowledge of basic arms and explosives use, and elementary military tactics, they are more likely to have acquired their skills from the Internet and in local gyms or national military service.

What is undoubtedly the most conscientious and comprehensive recent analysis of the matter was published in October 2009 by the Foreign Policy Research Institute in Philadelphia and presented in testimony before the Senate Foreign Relations Committee in Washington on October 7, 2009. Its author, Marc Sageman, is a medical doctor and psychiatrist who served as a U.S. Navy flight surgeon before joining the CIA, for which between 1987 and 1991 he was in Islamabad and New Delhi directing the U.S. multilateral program with the Afghan mujahideen. He has since held academic positions as well as returning to the practice of medicine.

The most recent of his works on terror networks and jihad groups is this comprehensive survey of al Qaeda activities since its founding, prepared in a collaborative project with the U.S. Secret Service, the New York City Police Department, and consultations with other American and foreign security and intelligence sources. The document (or Senate testimony) should be consulted in its whole (www.fpri.org), but those of its findings of particular interest here are that in the past two decades there have been sixty planned attacks (or "plots") in the West by al Qaeda or groups linked to it, and three have succeeded. (His analysis antedates the Christmas Day 2009 attempt to destroy an Amsterdam–Detroit passenger airliner.) Marc Sageman lists three categories of terrorist groups associated with al Qaeda: the core organization itself; self-organized autonomous groups having one or more members who are or have been in contact with al Qaeda, or had some form of training with it; and spontaneous copycat groups with no contact or training with al Qaeda.

The first attack in the West was the 1993 original attack on the World Trade Center in New York City by means of a truck with explosives placed in an underground parking space. The most recent (at the time the study was published) was a planned attack on the headquarters of the French General Directorate of Internal Security just outside Paris (whose planner was arrested before the attack took place). Of the sixty plots, all but one have been solved, and that one's plan and would-be perpetrators are mostly known.

Al Qaeda itself was directly linked to 20 percent of these sixty episodes. Most—78 percent of them—were the work of "autonomous homegrown groups" with no real connection to al Qaeda, but nevertheless its admirers and emulators, usually inspired to act by the U.S. invasion of Iraq.

Of the sixty "neo-jihad" plots in the West, nine were actually 1990s Algerian militant bombings in Paris, revenge for the French government's support for the military government then in power in Algeria. Three were al Qaeda's own successes (the 9/11 attacks, the London Transport bombings, and—indirectly, as al Qaeda people did not take part—the Madrid train bombings). Thirty-six other planned attacks were disrupted by police arrests, and ten failed because of mechanical or organizational incompetence by the terrorists.

The al Qaeda core organization became active in the West in 1993 (the first World Trade Center attack), peaked in 2001 with the 9/11 bombings, and since has appeared in decline. Excluding war casualties or victims claimed by groups calling themselves al Qaeda, only two other attacks were successful: in London and Madrid. Some three thousand Americans and others were killed on 9/11; fifty-two people died in London, and 191 died in Madrid.

According to the Foreign Policy Research Institute study, there has since been no "resurgent al Qaeda" in the West. The overall pattern of international terrorism since 2001 is increasingly that of a "leaderless jihad," resembling the spontaneous series of terrorist actions and murders of heads of state in Europe and America that were carried out more than a century ago by autonomous utopian anarchists.

Al Qaeda's relations with the Taliban today are troubled.

According to Sageman, any "Taliban return to power in Afghanistan will not mean an automatic new sanctuary for al Qaeda." He concludes that "effective counter-terrorism strategy [is] on the brink of completely eliminating al Qaeda," the result of effective international and domestic intelligence cooperation and good police work. No armies were involved.

Various "terrorist plots" announced by security officials have usually turned out to be inspired by bounty hunters and involve people manifestly incapable of the crimes they professedly intended to commit. One group in Miami offered to blow up the tallest building in the United States if their secret FBI interlocutor would identify the building and tell them in what city it was located, finance their transport, and counsel them on where to find explosives. In Canada a so-called "Toronto 18" terrorist cell turned out to contain no one who could name the Canadian prime minister the group intended to murder. Senior al Qaeda cadres, such as Abu Musab al-Suri, have complained that recruits from Europe were treating the training camps as a way to cleanse themselves after having "spent time with a whore in Bangkok." Not long after 9/11 a recruiting document found in a Paris mosque said: "[Jihad] is better than a holiday in Los Angeles! It's adventure!" A young Frenchman trained in Afghanistan during the same period said he "wanted to learn about guns, test his physique and get close to war without taking too many risks." A man involved in a scheme to blow up nightclubs in Britain thought that a camp in Pakistan would be like something he'd seen on television, with assault courses and rifle ranges, but "it wasn't like that at all." These examples are all from a recent issue of the London magazine *Prospect* (April 2009), which also notes that few of the would-be heros had more than sketchy notions of religion.

The two major attacks on public transport in Europe, in London and Madrid, have been claimed by "spokesmen" for al Qaeda, but police in Britain and Spain have denied that evidence exists to actually link the principals to that organization. Its adherents have carried out attacks on U.S. embassies in East Africa and on the destroyer USS *Cole*, in harbor in Yemen. The movement obviously is active in Afghanistan and in Pakistan, but there is no published evidence that it is the sophisticated global organization possessing the power to carry out attacks at will that it has been reputed to be.

In Britain, Italy, Spain, France, and the Balkans, the Muslims arrested for terrorist action or planning have consistently proven to be local, usually non-Arab, mainly alienated Maghrebi, Pakistani, or Bosnian young men from the Muslim immigration. The reputation of the movement is largely sustained by the press, spurred on by official alarms—during the Bush years, usually timed to coincide with elections or poor showings in domestic political polls. There has been doubt about how real the connection was between the actual al Qaeda in the tribal areas of Pakistan and the self-proclaimed al Qaeda "of Mesopotamia" in Iraq, whose ruthless tactics seem to have alienated rather than recruited Iraqis. Fundamentalist militants active for decades in Algeria, conducting a savage but unsuccessful campaign against military-dominated Muslim governments, gave themselves international notoriety and a new identity among Muslims by calling themselves "al Qaeda of the Islamic Maghreb." The same must be said of the newly self-proclaimed "al Qaeda of the Arabian peninsula" in Yemen, which claimed responsibility for the 2009 Christmas Day attempt to bomb an American passenger airliner arriving in Detroit from Amsterdam. During the past half century northern and southern Yemeni tribes have been at war, at various times identifying themselves as Nationalist, or Arab Socialist and Nasserite, or as a Marxist People's Republic. Now they can claim an al Qaeda emirate. "Plus ça change plus c'est la même chose," as the French say. In the Mali desert in West Africa, according to a *New York Times* report in 2008, "as many as two hundred fighters" from al Qaeda of the Islamic Maghreb pose "the biggest potential threat" confronting an American military mission which was then providing counterterrorism training (and job training!) to young Muslim men—the new U.S. Army Africa Command at work.*

There also is evidence that one reason Muslim support for al Qaeda has faded has been moral repugnance at its killing of bystanders and the innocent. A group of what the Pew Global Attitudes Project considers representative Muslim populations (including inside Israel and the Palestinian Territories) indicate that there was in 2003 an average 37.3 percent "confidence" in Osama bin Laden to "do the right thing." In 2008 the same figure was 11 percent. American

* *New York Times International Supplement*, October 3, 2008.

students of the history of terrorism in Europe and Ireland, such as Audrey Kurth Cronin of the National War College in Washington, describe a characteristic arc of commitment and activism in terrorist organizations, which suggests that al Qaeda is now on the declining side of the curve. Officials argue that if it were to be left unmolested in a territory of its own, as was the case in Afghanistan in 2001, it might regroup. However, this invites comparative analysis of the actual threat presented by such an isolated group, acting under serious external restraints, as against the costs and losses of the present American and NATO attempt to "clear and hold" Afghanistan (and, who knows—Pakistan and Yemen as well) against the movement.

Afghanistan is a nation of 251,773 square miles (652,090 square kilometers) with a population of some 22 million people, according to the current *Statesman's Yearbook* (London). Pakistan consists of 307,293 square miles (796,059 square kilometers) with a population of somewhat more than 141 million people. For comparison, the two add up to a territory nearly twice the size of united Germany, with twice Germany's population. The strategy for Afghanistan proposed by the United States Army in October 2009 was to "clear and hold" the territories disputed by the Taliban. To accomplish this in Afghanistan and extend it into the quasi-impenetrable tribal areas of Pakistan and those other areas of northern Pakistan where the Taliban have been active, or to separatist Balochistan, or in the worst case, to all of Pakistan (possibly provoking Indian intervention), seems an ambitious plan, to say the least.

It was always in the interest of the George W. Bush

administration to have al Qaeda seen as a global threat, since if it were not, the frustrating wars in Iraq and Afghanistan would be hard to explain. So would the former Bush administration's creation of its huge apparatus of international antiterrorism agencies, prisons, torture, and civilian surveillance as well as its massive domestic investment in "homeland defense"—which has seemed as ramshackle but profitable an undertaking as the American privatization of the actual wars in Iraq and Afghanistan, both of them seeming monuments to an unregulated American capitalism in decline.

The resemblances between modern Islamic radicalism and the efforts in earlier societies culturally threatened by the West to restore a golden age are obvious. An observer of the Taliban has called them not a revolutionary force themselves but the outcome of the revolutionary events of recent years. Such initiatives express the cultural frustrations of an elite and a people who feel themselves in a crucial way backward, unable to compete adequately with Western societies, victims of a political impotence responsible for the Arabs' failure to establish a successful political successor to the Ottoman system—an "Arab Nation" to take its place. The violence and religious radicalism produced in recent years in the Islamic world may, as I have argued, prove a transient, if tragic, phenomenon, neither unprecedented nor specific to the present period, as we have seen.

It is essential to distinguish between the radicalized and militant fundamentalist movements primarily of Arab origin, such as al Qaeda, and the Taliban—the fundamentalist "students of theology," who are drawn from a Pashtun ethnic population of some forty million that dominates a Central Asian region centered on northern Pakistan and Afghanistan (where Uzbek, Tajik, Turkmen, and other ethnic groups from neighboring states are also important presences).

The Obama administration chose, when it assumed office in 2009, to make the Taliban its primary enemy, identifying the crucial battlefield as no longer Iraq (possibly a rash assumption) but Afghanistan—and increasingly Pakistan as well. Bruce Riedel, an Afghanistan-Pakistan policy adviser to the Obama government, has described Pakistan as potentially posing "the most serious threat to the United States since the Soviet Union."[15] The conflated whole now is seen in Washington as what Donald Rumsfeld, in the immediate aftermath of the 9/11 attacks, identified as "a global insurrection" that the United States must defeat. The London-based Indian writer Pankaj Mishra, an eyewitness to the Central Asian crisis, compares the U.S.-NATO effort in Afghanistan with Richard Nixon's pursuit of "peace with honor" in Vietnam, which "primarily consisted of devastating Cambodia in addition to Vietnam." He adds, "For some years now, maintaining honor in Afghanistan has amounted to little more than the Talibanization of nuclear-armed Pakistan."[16]

At the time of the Taliban's rise, it was possible to understand Pakistan's support for them as a strategic investment in creating a readily manipulated satellite state in Kabul, and the support they enjoyed among the Afghan people as a political and cultural reaction to the violence and civil struggles of Afghanistan before and after the creation of a

pro-Soviet regime in 1978 and the subsequent Russian invasion. The Taliban-governed Afghanistan, as it existed before
2001, resembled a backward Wahhabi Saudi Arabia: It was
a rigid and aggressively reactionary integrist society and
theocratic government, much influenced by Pashtun tribal
custom and less sophisticated than the Saudis after the latter's long history of dealing with Americans and Westerners. Women were repressed and were denied education; the
regime was ignorant and xenophobic and practiced intellectual oppression and a comprehensive iconoclasm extending
to the destruction of the country's pre-Muslim monuments
from an earlier Buddhist civilization.

A Pakistani observer, Rafia Zakaria, writing in the the *Fri-
day Times* of Lahore,* has argued that the British colonial
period amputated a portion of Pakistan's history, cutting
society off from its past. The Taliban are responding to this
sentiment of a lost history by rejecting anything contemporary that is not authentically Pakistani and Muslim. Posi-
tioning themselves as the antithesis of modernity validates
their integrity. "Their rejection of modernity has become a
way to renew with our history, such as it might have occurred without the ignominy of British conquest." This is
not to be seen as a return to the past but as a positive creation. Their leaders make no secret of their formal ignorance and they mock legal procedures and classical Islamic
jurisprudence: they have no scruples about choosing that
Qur'anic law they think suits the case being judged.

---

* Reprinted in *Courrier International* (Paris) No. 965, April 10–May 6,
2009.

"Notions of grace and equity, much more frequent in the sacred texts, are conveniently ignored. Knowledge of religious and political formalities is overtly suspect, and power is sought in visible and visceral bodily submission. They are not a medieval survival but an entirely postmodern creation of rebellion against both modernity and rationality."

The Taliban's support by Pakistan places a strategically important border area under Pakistan's influence and weakens India's influence in Central Asia and, indirectly, in Kashmir. After al Qaeda's expulsion from its original installation in Sudan, under U.S. pressures, it had been afforded protection by the Taliban government in Afghanistan, with the approval of Pakistan, which saw the presence of foreign Islamists among the Taliban as providing a potential source of recruits for the underground struggle in Kashmir against India—always the principal preoccupation of Pakistan governments. This of course explains Pakistan's persistent resistance to American demands that the Pakistan army give priority to the American interest in destroying al Qaeda; Pakistan's own interest lies in manipulating both Taliban and foreign Islamist elements—as well as the United States, when feasible—in its own defense against its permanent enemy, India. The last motive became even more pressing when the George W. Bush administration chose to establish a special alliance and cooperative nuclear relationship with India without, it would seem, appreciating the complexities of the situation into which it was blundering. Nor, it would seem, does the Obama administration understand.

MOST AUTHORITIES ON Afghanistan and its history never-theless would probably have judged that without United States involvement, the Taliban would have proven a tran-sient political and social phenomenon in Afghanistan's long history and would have likely sooner or later succumbed to the influence of more liberal versions of Islam and been weakened by the rival communal interests of the other major ethnic communities in the country, including Tajiks, Hazaras, Uzbeks, and, of course, non-Taliban Pashtuns. This may yet prove the eventual outcome. The condition of Af-ghanistan at the time its Taliban leaders gave hospitality to Osama bin Laden and his associates, in flight from Sudan, was such that the decision seemed in Washington of rela-tively little significance (given that the Pakistani army was presumed to be in ultimate control of the situation). It might also have been thought that any risk presented by al Qaeda was under observation by Western intelligence agencies (it certainly was by the CIA) and could have been contained af-ter 9/11 by sensibly limited Western policies, without an in-vasion of Afghanistan that destroyed a considerable part of such national infrastructure as had survived the Soviet pe-riod and killed thousands of hapless Afghan civilians and Taliban soldiers innocent of any acquaintance with the exis-tence of either al Qaeda or the United States of America.

Neither of the two American deployments in Afghanistan, that in 2001 and today's renewed search for Osama bin Laden and his headquarters, seems even to have located him, or to have placed him at any risk of being attacked or seized. The vain pursuit of bin Laden has grossly inflated the reputation of al Qaeda and made him an international celebrity as

seeming leader of all radical Islam's resistance and coun-
teroffensive to the "aggressions" of the "New Crusaders"
and "Great Satan," and of course of the Zionists.

I SEEM TO be one of the very few Americans who do not believe in the enormity of the Islamic radical threat. I think
the violent cultural and religious radicalism of recent years
in the Islamic world is a passing phenomenon, neither unprecedented nor specific to the present period other than as
an aspect of events connected to the strategic competition
for the oil resources of Iran and the Middle East and the creation of a Jewish homeland in Palestine.

There is little new in what is happening. Colonial and
postcolonial history are filled with conflict between the ex-
panding and expansive West and the societies they were
attempting, usually successfully, to overrun. We have redis-
covered all this since the Second World War because one of
the most important—possibly the most important—results
of the war was the destruction of the European empires.
They were under attack on the left by the awakening and
newly sophisticated nationalists of the imperial territories, many of whom had been called to Europe in 1914—
the Indochinese laborers, Algerian and Moroccan ground
troops, Chinese labor battalions—and again in the Second
World War, when Charles De Gaulle's "Free French" army
was mostly composed of regular colonial troops from Central Africa whose leaders opted for De Gaulle rather than
the Vichy regime of Marshal Pétain, and from French North
Africa after the British and American invasion of Algeria

and Morocco in 1942. The British desert war against Italian forces and Rommel's Afrika Korps was fought in considerable part by regulars from the (colonial) Indian Army and by Australians and New Zealanders en route to Britain to fight in Europe. When Japan attacked in the Pacific, these colonial troops were sent home when transport allowed, but there were still some of them who landed in Normandy in 1944. The second "world" war was much more of a world war than we generally acknowledge. What Huntington has taken as a war between Islamic and Western civilizations is a matter of much deeper human forces.

The American political philosopher Mark Lilla claims that theological ideas as such "still inflame the ideas of man, stirring up messianic passions that leave societies in ruins."[17] I would think it obvious that it was not theological but secular utopian passions that were responsible for the Second World War and its totalitarian devastation, and that similar ideas, currently held in Washington and some other capitals, have already demonstrated, and continue to demonstrate, a similar capacity for the ruin of societies, not least their own.

VI

How It Ends

THE SECOND WORLD WAR and the Cold War were the final struggles among the surviving great powers of that era of revolution that began in Philadelphia in 1776 and Paris in 1789 and was closed by Mikhail Gorbachev's decision two centuries later that Russians must speak the truth to one another about the society in which they had lived for the preceding seven decades.

Another era had begun, in which the United States would be the dominant power, the nation that emerged from the great war of nations in 1914–1918 and the greater war of ideologies in 1939–1945 with its nationalism and ideology triumphant. President Jimmy Carter made two decisions that both precipitated and confirmed the collapse of the Soviet Union, while inadvertently preparing the conflicts between Islam and the United States that were to follow. He agreed to the proposal of his national security adviser, Zbigniew Brzezinski, to deliberately provoke a Soviet invasion of Afghanistan, intended to create Moscow's "own Vietnam

war"; and the president authorized a program by which
Saudi Arabia and Pakistan recruited an international force
of Muslim fighting men, motivated by religion, to fight that
Soviet invasion. The unforeseen consequences remain with
us today.[1]

During the Carter and Reagan administrations there was
a third development of great importance to the future. The
Pentagon was authorized to develop an international system of American regional military commands and bases,
implicitly the organizational infrastructure for American
world military domination. The George W. Bush presidency
further expanded and extended the scope of U.S. military
deployment following the 9/11 attacks, with the American
invasions of Afghanistan and Iraq. It issued the first in a series of National Security Strategy documents mandating
U.S. military superiority over the combined forces of all
possible challengers to the United States, the latest of which
is expected to be published in 2010.

President Ronald Reagan, the most naive and genial
imaginable representative of American nationalism and ideology, ordered large-scale rearmament and preparation for
space wars, while simultaneously affirming to Mikhail Gorbachev the ideal of complete nuclear disarmament.

President George H. W. Bush intelligently and successfully negotiated the termination of the Cold War. He also
inaugurated a new series of American Middle Eastern military engagements with the Gulf War against Iraq, a superficially comprehensible decision, at the same time one whose
deep sources remain today without a satisfactory explanation.
He also insisted upon the creation of an American base

complex in Saudi Arabia, the location of Islam's holiest places. The existence of this permanent installation of infidels in the Muslim Holy Land was avowedly what provoked Osama bin Laden to organize his attacks on New York City and Washington in 2001.

THE EMINENT AUSTRIAN economist and political philosopher Joseph Schumpeter wrote in his 1951 book *Imperialism and Social Classes,* that imperialism

> necessarily carries the implication of an aggressiveness, the true reasons for which do not lie in the aims which are temporarily being pursued; of an aggressiveness that is only kindled anew by each success; of an aggressiveness for its own sake, as reflected in such terms as "hegemony," "world dominion," and so forth. And history, in truth, shows us nations and classes—most nations furnish an example at one time or another—that seek expansion for the sake of expanding, war for the sake of fighting, victory for the sake of winning, dominion for the sake of ruling. This determination cannot be explained by any of the pretexts that bring it into action, by any of the aims for which it seems to be struggling at the time. . . . Expansion for its own sake always requires, among other things, concrete objects if it is to reach the action stage and maintain itself, but this does not constitute its meaning. Such expansion is in a sense its own "object" . . . [2]

Fifty years ago, in connection with American postwar policy, it was possible to write of a "denatured imperialism" which invoked the phrase "world security" instead of "world dominion"—"dominion" indicating international responsibility without the concomitant obsession with war. This cannot be said today, as American foreign policy, economy, and society seem all to have become dominated by the assumptions of permanent or serial wars against American enemies, identified by Washington as the enemies as well of democracy and Western civilization. American officials have spoken of a generalized "insurrection" in the non-Western world against institutions and assumptions that reflect the influence of the United States.

Since the end of the American war in Indochina, the final component war of the Cold War, the American government has carried out military interventions into the Dominican Republic, Grenada, Panama, and (by intermediaries) in Cuba and Nicaragua, as well as in Somalia (partly under UN auspices) and in Bosnia and Serbia (to support the NATO Europeans, who had a UN "protection" mandate). It has fought in Iraq (twice); and in Afghanistan for the past nine years (with, at this writing, ancillary operations in Pakistan that imply an attempt to establish control of the hitherto quasi-impenetrable and unconquerable Pashtun tribal areas, and to force the Pakistan government to conduct military action to suppress domestic terrorism).

The United States recently could scarcely be said to be conducting a "denatured" imperialism without war, but rather to have been conducting wars for an unacknowledged or undeclared or even unimagined empire—unimagined in that the mass of Americans would reject or even recoil from the notion of a formal empire. It is not popular ambition that drives American policy, but the assumptions and beliefs of an American elite concerned with foreign policy, which has a particular sense of an American international mission to use the nation's power to establish a new international order, congenial to their notions of international as well as national destiny. This will assure America's permanent access to oil and natural gas, reinforce the place of the United States in world history, and identify the elite as responsible figures in this achievement. Andrew Bacevich has described American foreign policy as "having long been the province of a small, self-perpetuating, self-anointed group of specialists . . . dedicated to the proposition of excluding democratic influences from the making of national security policy. To the extent that members of the national security apparatus have taken public opinion into consideration, they have viewed it as something to manipulate."[3]

I do not consider material interest an adequate explanation for the conduct of governments and nations, least of all the American, although I do not underestimate the importance of access to energy and material gain in the currents influencing policy in every world capital. Nonetheless, fundamental motives must be looked for in the intellectual and moral realms of national decision, and in the vulnerability of people—intellectuals and political professionals notably among them—to the vulgarization of ideas in political ideology, which, as the twentieth century demonstrated, can justify nearly anything—even the most outrageous (as measured by the norms of ordinary rationality).

The proposition that the United States can or should devote the next fifteen, or fifty, years to "making" modern nations of Afghanistan or Pakistan, by means of a massive introduction into those countries of American officials, advisors, and teachers, as well as of soldiers to suppress military uprising or resistance to such an effort, at first proposed by the G. W. Bush administration, seems to me not ignoble, but simply breathtakingly ignorant, impractical, indifferent to historical experience and the political limits on nations, and contrary to the will as well as the interests of the peoples involved.* I would think that existing public support—or toleration—in the United States for such a project comes from the manipulation of that morbid fear that has been part of the American mood since 9/11.

The "Long War" was actually going on well before George W. Bush promised to rid the world of tyranny. Since the Vietnam withdrawal, the United States has repeatedly been at war, yet with two exceptions (the two Iraq invasions, in neither of which was the Iraqi army disposed to fight), it has never fought a regular army, nor—rarely noted—has it ever since 1945 won a war, other than the

---

* A December 22, 2009, report in the *International Herald Tribune* said there already were nearly 1,000 American civilian volunteers in Afghanistan, and soon would be 1,200 to 1,300 as part of a "civilian surge" to improve the lives of Afghanis. This is "the most ambitious civilian campaign" in a foreign country "in a generation." Their mission, officials said, is to stabilize Afghanistan, and "will require cleaning up its government, weaning its farmers from poppy cultivation, making its people healthier, even teaching them to read." Afghanistan's estimated present population is well over the 1994 official figure of 20.5 million, most of it illiterate.

invasion of the Dominican Republic, the pathetic conquest of Panama, and the successful seizure of that menacing member of the British Commonwealth, the Caribbean island nation of Grenada. It has not won a clear victory against a serious opponent since the Second World War. It failed to do so in the Korean War and in Vietnam. Its enemies have nearly always been dissenting political movements, guerrillas, insurgents, terrorists—which is to say civilians, acting within civilian society ("hiding behind civilians," as Israelis as well as Americans claim when these enemies employ violence, "thereby forcing us to kill civilians").[4]

The commitment of the American government, or, to be more exact, of its political, foreign policy, and military elite, to semipermanent but unsuccessful war against changing enemies in the non-Western world has maintained public support by the identification of each enemy in turn as (to use the expression the Israelis like to use) an "existential" threat to America, or as contributing to such a threat. The Asian Communists had to be fought in Indochina so that Chinese political agents or armies would not overrun Asia with all its resources and manpower, isolating the West. Fighting them there would save Americans from fighting them at home. It is the same with "Islamic terrorists." British prime minister Gordon Brown, speaking for NATO as well as Britain, used that exact phrase during the summer of 2009, while visiting British troops in Afghanistan. He said that NATO's soldiers had been mobilized to fight in Afghanistan so that the terrorists (or the Taliban) would not have to be fought at home. The Australian analyst David Kilcullen, an anthropologist and former officer in his own country's army, advisor to U.S. generals Stanley McChrystal and David Petraeus, and a Pentagon consultant, discusses in a recent book the likelihood of a fifty- to one-hundred-year counterinsurgency campaign to defeat a global network of Islamic revolutionaries who want to conquer the West.*

What lies behind this? The material interests involved in the Middle East are obvious, of course, but they do not explain the element of unreasonableness present. In what respect, for example, was Saddam Hussein "a threat to the world," as former Prime Minister Tony Blair described him on January 30, 2010, to the formal inquiry the government had ordered into the origins of Britain's participation in the invasion of Iraq in 2003? The George W. Bush administration's invasion first of Afghanistan and then of Iraq constituted decisive developments in international relations. The period that began in the supreme drama of the 9/11 New York and Washington attacks was exploited by the Bush administration to support longstanding conservative American as well as Israeli foreign policy objectives (Iraq's and Iran's disarmament, with development of Iraq as a U.S. strategic base). This was accompanied by the effort of the president and vice president to establish a novel conception of "wartime" executive power as subsuming or overriding existing legislative and judicial power in the United States, as well as established common law, amounting to a challenge to the

---

* *The Accidental Guerrilla: Fighting Small Wars in the Midst of a Big One* (New York: Oxford University Press, 2009).

traditional interpretation of the American constitutional division of powers.

The Yale historian John Lewis Gaddis wrote soon after the al Qaeda attacks on the World Trade Center and Pentagon that they had shattered "the boundaries between everyday existence and a dangerous world." He compared this with the British attack on Washington and burning of the Capitol in 1814, events that he said had confirmed the wisdom of the policy of isolating the American nation from Europe, recommended by the nation's founders.

He did not, however, commend the founders' wisdom to President Bush; instead he approvingly compared George Bush's invasion of Iraq in 2003 with the actions of successive American presidents after 1814, characterized by Gaddis as "preemption, unilateralism, and hegemony." Annexation of Spanish Florida, expulsion of the Seminole Indians across the Mississippi, annexation of Texas, war with Mexico, and seizure of California and the "derelict territories" of present-day Arizona, New Mexico, Colorado, Utah, and Nevada were all meant, according to Gaddis, to preempt threats and install democracy. It was destiny.[5]

The invasion of Afghanistan in 2001 was unsuccessful in capturing the al Qaeda leaders but was successful in destroying the reactionary and repressive Taliban government in Kabul, which had provided refuge to the kindred Islamist al Qaeda movement after the United States had forced the latter's expulsion from Sudan. The invasion of Iraq in 2003—as soon became evident—was primarily to unseat Saddam Hussein, who had nothing to do with al Qaeda or the 9/11 attacks, and to install in Iraq a major American strategic base and a friendly elected government that might inspire a move-ment toward representative government throughout the region.

One could think that the wars and military interventions of the United States in Southwest and Central Asia and the Middle East since 2001 have been directed by American leaders and ratified by the public as what might be called a homeopathic or symbolic response to a generalized fear of the disorders that had come to be seen as threats newly de-veloping in the world beyond the known terrain of the Cold War, NATO Europe, Japan, and the established Amer-ican security sphere in Israel and Saudi Arabia. Beyond that is where President Bush's "terror" (or "Evil") dwells and must be fought. Since the Cold War's end to 9/11 there were no specific military threats to North America or NATO Europe of any gravity. The Yugoslav wars posed no threat beyond the Balkans. Terrorist attacks do not jeopard-ize national existence. Even since 2001 the only significant threats have been virtual (a nuclear Iran, the fear of terror-ist mass-destruction weapons, the nightmare of a new global caliphate ruled by fanatical Arabs). Militarism is the domination of the military in society, an undue deference to military demands, and an emphasis on military consider-ations, spirit, ideals, and scales of value, in the lives of states. "It has meant also the imposition of heavy burdens on a people for military purposes, to the neglect of welfare and culture, and the waste of a nation's best manpower in un-productive army service." I quote the definition of the dis-tinguished modern historian of militarism ("civilian and military," as he notes) Alfred Vagts (1892–1986). He served in the German army in the First World War emigrating to the United States before the Second, to an appointment at the Institute for Advanced Studies at Princeton.

There were aspects of militarism evident in the European professional armies of the pre-Westphalian period (indeed the Assyrian army of antiquity was a fighting organization of great efficiency, complete with Imperial Life Guards, chaplains, and an emphasis on "smartness"—a distinctly militarist quality). However, the term entered the modern political vocabulary together with the imperialism as a term of abuse during the French Second Empire (1852–1870). The republican and socialist enemies of the government applied the two epithets to the rule of Napoleon III, which embraced the Crimean War, the French-Piedmontese war with Austria, from which France withdrew after the battle of Solferino (1859), the Mexican imperial adventure (from which the United States ousted Napoleon's brother-in-law, Maximilian, in 1866), and the war with Prussia and capitulation of the Second Empire at Sedan in 1870.

Imperialism and militarism are coeval because both are concerned with extending domination, the first over an enlarged territory, and the latter to increase state power (meaning men and funds for the army). "The two hardly ever exist by themselves. Both are tendencies largely 'justified' by history—that is, they cover their demands with a cloak of tradition . . ."

Vagts distinguished militarism from military science, the professional practice of wartime strategy and tactics to obtain victory. "Modern militarism has, nonetheless, specific traits," and is vulnerable to narcissism. An army so built that it serves military men's ambition rather than war is militaristic; "so is everything in an army which is not preparation for fighting, but merely exists for diversion or to satisfy peacetime whims like the long-anachronistic cavalry." (A contemporary accusation could be made that the United States Air Force and Navy both display instances of this narcissism. The former does so with its obsession with aircraft so technologically advanced as to be useless in contemporary war, such as the B-1 bomber and the F-22 fighter—obsolescent in that they exist to counter Soviet weapons systems that never were and never will be built. The Navy, as William Lind, a prominent military theorist, notes, maintains eleven large aircraft carrier battle groups "structured to fight the Imperial Japanese Navy [although] submarines are today's and tomorrow's capital ships; the ships that most directly determine the control of blue waters."[6]

The American national elections in 2006 and 2008 had as their main issue whether to continue the wars in Iraq, or in Iraq and Afghanistan (and Pakistan, since by 2008 the possibility of intervention or incursion into that country was clearly visible). In 2006 and 2008 the electorate voted for withdrawal from Iraq, and in 2008 it gave Barack Obama an ambiguous mandate concerning Afghanistan, endorsing the continued pursuit of al Qaeda (after eight years of that group's successful defiance of the United States) on Mr. Obama's promise that while closing down the Iraq war he would prosecute the "right" war in Afghanistan, but without clarifying his intentions with respect to the Taliban in both Afghanistan and Pakistan. Both cases posed issues of "regime change" to which he seemed to have given little serious thought.

The election of 2008 brought into office a sympathetic new president, internationally appreciated, more open to dialogue with opponents than his predecessors, but under immensely powerful political pressures not to change existing security policy. These were reinforced in Congress by the overwhelming force of Pentagon institutional thinking and Pentagon-allied industrial interests, as well as the influence of that vast majority of the professional foreign policy community in Washington and academic circles who accept the current ideology. The housing for the hundreds if not thousands of new personnel for the new civilian as well as military "surge" to "reform" and remake Afghanistan's (and conceivably Pakistan's) government (and "way of life") was already being purchased, and the American personnel assigned to the task were being trained even before Barack Obama's election.

No doubt it was on the recommendations of Defense Secretary Robert Gates and Central Command commandant General David Petraeus that the new president named General Stanley McChrystal to the Afghanistan command and sent him to Kabul to assess the situation. On his return the general produced a plan already drafted by the ascendant Petraeus-led faction in the Pentagon, which enjoys the support of the so-called "clear and hold" program, used successfully in Malaya by the British after the Second World War (when the insurgency against the Malay majority was based in the Chinese minority, supported from Communist China), and again, unsuccessfully, late in the war in Vietnam.*

There was in fact no reason to expect President Obama to do otherwise than follow McChrystal's recommendations. Wholly lacking military experience, preoccupied by the world economic crisis and his legislative campaign for health care reform, Mr. Obama already had accepted the interpretation of the Afghanistan and Pakistan situation generally held in Washington and the press. Indeed, his campaign advisers had proposed a considerably exaggerated version of the dominant Washington scenario, emphasizing the risk of Pakistan's nuclear weapons falling into terrorist hands (and seemingly deaf to the risk of powerful Pakistani popular as well as official reactions against U.S. interference in the country's affairs.)†

The future of the war in Central Asia is generally presumed in military (as well as critical civilian) assessments to involve American energy and pipeline interests, although it requires optimism to plan major infrastructure projects in the chaotic conditions that now seem likely to prevail for a

---

* This military faction believes that the United States' Vietnam defeat was caused by a "stab in the back" by the press and television in the 1960s–1970s, by Congress, and by the Nixon administration, which negotiated an agreement with Hanoi by which the United States abandoned that war at just the moment when, in these military critics' view, victory had become possible.

† See, for example, Bruce Riedel, "Armageddon in Islamabad," *National Interest*, Washington, July–August 2009. Riedel forecast a terrorist threat to nuclear-armed Pakistan that would be "felt around the globe." Riedel, formerly of the CIA, was an adviser to the Obama campaign and is now at the Brookings Institution.

long time to come. In searching for the motives for American policy it seems to me profitable to recall Schumpeter's "expansion for its own sake," always in need of pretexts to justify it.

A deep change has taken place in the nature of American government, creating a solid obstacle to the effort to carry out actions that would seem so obviously appealing to public opinion as to end a vast war of obscure relevance to citizens and of distressing prospects. The nature of American government itself has changed during the two decades since the Reagan administration, inviting private or corporate influence and participation in the making and execution of foreign and military policy.[7]

Energy is not the only American industrial interest involved. The "war against terror," in an era of privatized governmental functions, has been enormously profitable to many American corporations. It is reported by the Pentagon that in the second quarter of 2009 the number of private security contractors working in Iraq for the American military rose by 23 percent, and in Afghanistan by 29 percent, so that private contractors, which is to say private American business, now provides half the American armed force and military activity in those countries, constituting a privatization of war and transformation of it into a profit-center for corporate enterprise that is without precedent. This augments the enormous scale of American government spending today on past and future armaments, including hyper-technological weaponry of scarcely any imaginable utility short of a future invasion of the United States from Mars.

Certainly the American investment in global bases and in the technological means potentially to control space and cyberspace—or if they cannot be controlled or preemptively occupied, to deny military access to them by any other government or political actor—assumes potential or actual threats consistent only with some version of major war. Who will be the enemies? The only imaginable candidates are China, Russia, the European Union or one of its individual members (which is most implausible), or conceivably one of the larger developing states such as Brazil—or Pakistan.

The present level of American arms spending sustains the national economy (and increases national indebtedness) at a time of business and financial crisis resulting from the abandonment of (or release from) regulations and values that constrained financial recklessness in the past, notably Franklin Roosevelt's New Deal regulation of banking and markets, and regulations dating from the Progressive Era at the end of the nineteenth century and the early twentieth century.

American business in the past also functioned in a culture of important religious influence and an Anglo-Saxon ethos of chivalric service and obligation, as expressed, for example, in the correspondence and speeches of Theodore Roosevelt and Woodrow Wilson (and incidentally, in the philosophical writings of Adam Smith). These articulated the values of a Protestant elite, and notions of public obligation, that despite their inevitable hypocrisies provided an important influence on the governing classes in the United States.

In the Second World War, General of the Army George C.

Marshall, army chief of staff and later Harry S. Truman's secretary of state, never wore on his uniform the decorations and service ribbons to which his First World War service entitled him. He said that it would be unseemly for him, working in a Washington office, to wear honors deserved by the young men he was responsible for sending into battle. (Compare U.S. general officers today, who even when wearing combat camouflage are decorated like operetta supernumeraries.) Following the war, Marshall was offered a million (1945) dollars for his memoirs, but he refused, saying that it would not be correct for him to profit from his public duties. This ethic was reflected in public behavior until, I suppose, the time of Vietnam—implicated in so much that has gone bad in the United States.

The prevailing ethical norms of American business came to an end partially under the influence of academic and professional innovations that declared ethical values to be exogenous obstacles to policies essential to maximum economic efficiency, and that made the elevation of return on capital the determinant of business and industrial success, excluding as inefficiencies earlier norms of duty to community, workforce, and public interest. It is difficult to say to what extent American policy makers really did, or do, believe that a global democratic order is advanced by the nation's current policies, as American policy has avowed, or even believe that it is possible. If you dispassionately state the policy's goals, which are "defeat" or suppression of an aggressively anti-Western fundamentalist religious movement throughout a considerable part of the approximately billion members of the Islamic religion, and winning such people over to political values and institutions (and necessarily to an outlook on the political role of religion) resembling those of Americans or Europeans, the policy possesses no credibility.

The current practical measures of the American Defense and State departments in reorganizing and redirecting the American military and civilian services toward the goals of rebuilding the political culture and institutions of the Muslim countries in which the United States is intervening nonetheless have this as their official purpose. As Robert W. Tucker and David C. Hendrickson have remarked (in *The National Interest*), fall 2005, such a policy of global "liberation" finds no support in the American Constitution, and such a policy alters the definition of threats to America from what other nations "do" to what they "are," thus redirecting foreign policy from the pursuit of limited and practical goals to unlimited action for nonmaterial and unachievable purposes (actually implying unending war).

The eminent economist (and U.S. ambassador to India during the Kennedy administration) the late John Kenneth Galbraith wrote in his 1999 memoir that "a major feature of our foreign policy [is] its institutional rigidity, which holds it on course even when it is visibly wrong. So it was on Vietnam, as is now accepted; so on . . . military alliances with the poor lands. So it is or was on such matters as the unnecessary enlargement of NATO or the continuing trade and travel sanctions on Cuba. . . ." So it remains.[8]

WAR IN THE post-Enlightenment age has reflected the Enlightenment's creation of a new intellectual and moral structure resting on human reason and commitment to science, and on the assumption, although not the evidence, of human moral progress. The sinister aspect of the phenomenon of secular utopianism, the twenty-first century's principal source of mass popular political mobilization, has been its association with a value-free scientific rationalism that lends itself to what in another day would have been yet considered objectively criminal political policies and practices, in recent times too often have found progressive justification.

Only since the early twentieth century have there been the scientific and technological means for gassing, burning, bombing, and otherwise destroying millions of civilians in an industrial manner, employing the bureaucratic and managerial resources of a modern state. Examples include the Nazi death camps; the aerial attacks on civilians during the last months of the Second World War that reached their crescendo in the deliberate ignition of fire-storms in German cities, designed to kill by sucking oxygen out of the air (and out of the victims themselves, leaving their corpses shriveled); and the devastating incendiary attacks on wooden Japanese cities. These constitute a Western moral inheritance that cannot be ignored. Even the atrocities of Maoism and Pol Pot's Cambodia incorporated elements of Western provenance, in Marxism-Leninism and its romantic elaboration in European radical circles during the mid-twentieth century.

Today, the United States is bound by its 2002 Strategic Offensive Treaty (SORT) with Russia to reduce its total number of deployed strategic weapons warheads to 2,200 by 2012 (tactical weapons are not included). In its most recent START (Strategic Arms Revelation Treaty) declaration, for 2003, the United States listed a total of 5,968 deployed nuclear weapons of all categories. What are these for?

In the ability of leaders to conceptualize and prepare the means for the annihilation of an enemy during the Second World War and the Cold War, and in plans for future wars, twentieth-century Western war has expressed, as never was possible before, the Faustian spirit of extreme and defiant ambition and extreme risk. The Enlightenment created a Western intellectual and moral structure that was expected to rest on reason, scientific knowledge, and secular progress, but in this matter notably does not.

American war in the past decade has itself changed in a fundamental respect. In the twentieth century it was defensive and, since at least the time of the war with Spain in 1898, was conceived in other terms than national self-aggrandizement. The Western—notably American—retention of nuclear weapons during the Cold War possessed a deterrent logic, but in the perpetuation and in some cases modernization of existing nuclear arsenals there would seem to be evident connection to unavowed fantasies of omnipotence, impossible to gratify but also impossible to renounce, linked to a pattern of secular utopianism or utopian nationalism.

THIS PATTERN ORDINARILY is meant to enforce a system of values held not only to embody the nation's virtues but to be of universal historical importance, a step toward a future that will provide a transformation of such importance that the existing system must be overturned and replaced, necessarily at a cost to existing international law and political and moral convention. After 9/11, American strategy was reconceived as preemptive and "preventive," the first denoting action against an imminent threat and the second meaning to eliminate a threat conceived to lie in the future. This characterized the George W. Bush presidency, and might reasonably be expected to return if, or when, a Republican administration replaces the present one.

In today's policy debate, Republicans generally as well as neoconservatives and a great many people from the liberal camp remain supporters of the idea that the world's destiny is democracy, so that this should be accounted the "strong trend" in contemporary history which a positive American policy should reinforce to its own advantage. It argues that there has been a steady trend toward the integration of nations and the development of cooperative institutions that can reasonably be expected eventually to end in a global order that resembles the traditional goals of American "Wilsonianism." This edifying ambition does not alter the fundamental moral nature of society as we have always known it.

In this respect a word must be said about the neoconservative influence on the Bush presidency. The neoconservatives assumed a place on the active American political right that had not before been occupied. At the time of Mr. Bush's election, the American right thereby empowered could be said to range from the vice president, Richard Cheney, with his corporate interests and connections, especially with the oil industry, to the so-called Christian right, a force of consequence in the Republican electorate and the Congress. This community included many with apocalyptic expectations about international developments inspired by what seem to them Biblical prophecies being fulfilled in events preceding the September 11, 2001, attacks on the United States—above all the founding of Israel and the return of Jews to Jerusalem.

These conservatives are all American in origin. The neoconservatives are, in part, the product of certain European currents of thought, notably by way of Leo Strauss, classicist and political philosopher of German origin who emigrated to the United States in 1938 and taught for many years at the University of Chicago, and Carl Schmitt, a German legal scholar and jurist who remained active in Germany during the Nazi period. Their influence was chiefly in emphasizing the primacy of the state as a national community in opposition to "others," in justifying exceptional and extreme uses of power to assure state security in times of crisis, and in their identification of American liberalism—especially in its 1968 American manifestation—as a force of national political and cultural decline.

Their view of the state has coincided with the position defended by the legal school of unitary executive power in American government, which had attracted attention if not notoriety before the Bush administration came to power, and whose disciples were appointed to major legal positions in his administration. The argument made by Bush administration lawyers that in times of war a president exercises

the totality of the government's executive power (the "unitary executive"), overriding existing legal and constitutional limits on that power, coincides with the position of
Carl Schmitt. This view of executive power rationalized the
president's authorization of torture in violation of established international and domestic law, and his radical position holding that "signing statements" by the executive can
override the intent or enforcement of Congressional law.
Many of the neoconservatives became Mr. Bush and his cab-
inet's counselors and were implementers of these White
House policies. Together, they furnished the intellectual
rationale for the use by the United States of its military
power and political resources to promote a new American-
led international order consistent with the apocalyptic view
they take of contemporary world affairs. The Straussians
hold that "moral clarity" is essential to counter the destructive liberalism inhibiting the state's necessary use of power
to sustain a necessary order in the West. They claim the
privilege of using deception to gain posts in which this clarity would serve the state. Claes G. Ryn of the Catholic University of America in Washington has accused them of a new
version of ideological Jacobism, in what he calls a conspiracy
against democracy as it actually exists in the United States.
He writes that part of the appeal of Strauss to his students
was his claim that

> only a few sophisticated minds can really under-
> stand and face the truth about politics. To protect
> themselves against the ignorant and to be able to

> influence the powers-that-be, the philosophers must, according to Strauss, hide their innermost beliefs and true motives, not least from rulers whom they want to advise. Following Plato's recommendation, they must tell "noble lies" that are more palatable to others than the truth . . . [9]

Since the 2008 presidential election the neoconservatives have been out of power in Washington, but they remain important members of the intellectual and political community that dominates Washington's international policy. They occupy "think-tank" and academic positions and have founded new institutions to combat the Obama administration. Christopher Caldwell, senior editor of the most important neoconservative magazine, Washington's *Weekly Standard*, characterized President Obama's speech in Cairo in June 2009 as "penitent, humbled and even sycophantic," the purpose of which, Caldwell felt, was to "break faith with Israel," an act of weakness as well as an acknowledgment that enemies now "have the upper hand" in what Caldwell (like other neoconservatives) continues to regard as a battle by the United States, "whether it likes it or not, . . ." for civilization's survival.[10]

THERE HAS ALWAYS been, and remains, a noninterventionist alternative to the foreign policy followed by the United States since the beginning of the 1960s. This would discard ideological and historicist generalizations, minimize interference in the affairs of other societies, and accept the existence of an international system of plural, legitimate, and autonomous powers and interests.*

It would emphasize pragmatic and empirical judgment of the interests and needs of the American nation, and of others. It would accept the realism of George Kennan's stark judgment that democracy along West European and American lines cannot prevail internationally. "To have real self-government, a people must understand what this means, want it, and be willing to sacrifice for it." Many nondemocratic systems are inherently unstable. "But so what?" Kennan asked in 1993. "We are not their keepers. We never will be." He did not anticipate that before his death, at the age of 101 in 2005, his country would have committed itself to a huge effort to become the world's "keeper." He recommended asking only from foreign nations, "governed or misgoverned as habit or tradition will dictate," that "their governing cliques observe, in their bilateral relations with the United States, and with the remainder of the world community, the minimum standards of civilized diplomatic intercourse."[11]

A policy of nonintervention would rely heavily on diplomacy and analytical intelligence, with particular attention

---

* Confusion is sometime produced because the "realist" and noninterventionist policy recommendations put forward in the 1950s and 1960s were at the time pejoratively called "neo-isolationist," which they were not (whatever that term may mean in contemporary practice). The possibility of a modern American isolationist foreign policy was exhaustively considered by the Brown University political scientist Eric A. Nordlinger in his 1995 book (pre-globalism and pre-9/11), *Isolationism Reconfigured: American Foreign Policy for a New Century*. It ends (unhelpfully) by recommending "moderated idealistic activism."

to history, since nearly all serious problems among nations are recurrent or have important recurring elements in them. Current crises concerning Iran, Afghanistan, Pakistan, Iraq, Lebanon, and Palestine-Israel all have origins in the European imperial systems and their dismantlement in the aftermath of the twentieth century's totalitarian wars. They are the legacy or in a sense the residue of the history of the last century, and their resolution must be sought in terms of that experience, a fact generally ignored in American political and press references to history—which, despite the frequent polemical citation of historical "lessons," is usually poorly known.

A noninterventionist American foreign policy requires a White House that will understand its primary responsibility to be the well-being and quality of American life. It would curtail nonessential external commitments and support multilateral methods and forums for dealing with international problems and crises, to the extent that this is useful. It would redefine its national security strategy narrowly so as to make its priorities the protection of the American polity and its constitutional government, and its security against military threat. It would reduce military expenditures to levels commensurate with the actual problems of the contemporary world and not the hypothetical threats of science fiction. It would regard nonstate threats of subversion and terrorism as primarily matters for the criminal police and other civilian agencies of security. It would honor the security guarantees given foreign nations and would make the well-being of states historically close to the United States, and to which it is allied by treaty, its con-

cern, but would cease to make military sales and assistance
routine instruments of American diplomacy. It is not in the
American interest to supply backward governments with
the weapons to fight one another, or to repress their own
populations.

Such a noninterventionist policy would rely primarily on
trade and the market, rather than on territorial control or
military intimidation, to provide the resources and energy
the United States needs. American security deployments
abroad would be reexamined with attention to whether they
might actually be impediments to solutions of the conflicts
of clients, or might empower civil war or nationalist irre-
dentism, as in Georgia and East Africa.

It would undertake the inevitably controversial reduction of America's global military command structure, recog-
nizing that too often it has been a provocation to nationalist
hostility towards to the United States and an inspiration to
radical forces and the extremist violence it is intended to
prevent—in practice a program that automatically gener-
ates its own contradiction.

It would assume that nations are responsible for their
own political affairs so long as these do not directly threaten
the larger interests of the international community. It would
act on the assumption that American intervention in others'
affairs, even when benevolent, is more likely to turn small
problems into big ones. This would seem a position attrac-
tive to an American public that traditionally has believed
in individual responsibility and the autonomy of markets,
considers itself hostile to political ideology (largely unaware
of its own), and professes to be governed by pragmatism,

compromise, and constitutional order. This was the case in the era of the republic's beginnings, but it no longer seems to be the national taste, or at least not that of its leadership.

HAD A NONINTERVENTIONIST policy been followed in the 1960s, there would have been no American war in Indochina. The struggle there would have been recognized as nationalist in motivation, unsusceptible to solution by foreigners, and inherently limited in its international consequences, whatever they might be—as proved to be the case. The United States would never have been defeated, its army demoralized, or its students radicalized. There would have been no American invasion of Cambodia and no Khmer Rouge genocide. Laos and its tribal peoples would have been spared their ordeal.

The United States would not have suffered its catastrophic implication in what was essentially a domestic crisis in Iran in 1979, which still poisons Near and Middle Eastern affairs, since there would never have been the Nixon administration's huge and provocative investment in the Shah's regime as America's "gendarme" in the region, compromising the Shah and contributing to that fundamentalist backlash against his secularizing modernization that provoked the Islamists' revolution.

Instead of a general assurance in his Cairo speech in June 2009, addressed to the Muslim world, that the United States intended to withdraw its troops from Iraq and Afghanistan and wished to have no bases there, to which there has been no sequel, President Barack Obama might have actually asked the governments of the region for their political assistance to the United States in accomplishing these desirable ends, as well as offering a withdrawal of American forces from South and Central Asia as a whole, and from the Middle East, whose well-being, manner of self-rule, and social and religious affairs might be considered of inherently limited importance to the United States and the affair of the peoples themselves rather than of Washington officials.

Without entering further into what could become a futile discussion of the "mights" or "might nots" of the last half-century, one can say that the United States would certainly not have found itself at war in 2010 in Afghanistan and Pakistan (and indirectly in Somalia, Yemen, and elsewhere in Africa), while still trying to extricate itself from the consequences of its invasion of Iraq seven years earlier.

Israel, with its conventional and unconventional arms, is capable of assuring its own defense against external aggression, even if newly aware of the limits of its ability to win victories against irregular local and foreign resistance to its occupation of the Palestinian territories which can only increase as its demographic disadvantage mounts. It cannot expect total security without political resolution of the Palestinian question, a problem only it can solve, presumably by withdrawing from the illegally occupied Palestinian territories. With the arrival of the Obama administration in Washington, Israel was once again urged to search for such a solution but was given no new incentive to do so. Forty years of past American involvement have mainly enabled, or indeed encouraged, the Israelis to avoid facing facts, facilitating its colonization of Palestine, accompanied by the emergence of quasi-fascist settler groups hostile to the Israeli government itself, all contributing to that radicalization of Islamic society that inspires a continuing search for revenge. The major shifts in Israeli public opinion and in government policy following the attack on Gaza in the winter of 2008–2009 produced the formation of a government encouraging further seizure of Palestinian territory, a policy inviting new resistance.[12] Elsewhere, a noninterventionist Washington might reasonably consider people who are victims of domestic despots, such as the Iraqis before 2003, to be responsible for their own solutions and usually capable of their own revolutions—if they really do want change or revolution. No foreign power occupied Iraq in 2003, imposing Saddam Hussein's dictatorship, and as 2010 began, the only foreign intervention in Afghanistan and Pakistan is America's (and NATO's).

This may be considered a hard-headed, or hard-hearted, doctrine concerning the responsibilities of people themselves, even shocking when international media audiences witness atrocities in Darfur and elsewhere. It does not necessarily imply passivity in the face of atrocity. The appalling nonintervention of the Western powers in Yugoslav ethnic cleansing during the initial UN intervention in that country in 1992 occurred because the Security Council (under U.S. pressure, motivated by Washington's unwillingness to get involved) pusillanimously limited the UN mission to "peace-keeping" even while a war of aggression was taking place. Only after the Bosnian Serbs attacked UN soldiers, taking prisoners, was military intervention decided by the

European governments involved, which the United States then insisted be placed under NATO command. The Dayton agreement that followed separated the combatants, but the situation of Kosovo, its Serbian minority population, and the Albanians of the region is still without a reliable settlement.

A noninterventionist foreign policy is entirely compatible with multilateral international reaction to atrocious public crimes and the existence of international criminal courts (which the United States has generally opposed because of its present vulnerability to indictments and prosecution for a number of practices that have been or are national policy). However, it is extremely difficult to conduct international interventions in such matters with more positive than negative results, since many such emergencies have causes beyond decisive international remedy. The ultimate roots of the Darfur crisis are ethnic and climatic, since many arable regions of sub-Saharan Africa are experiencing gradual desertification, which causes conflict between the agricultural peoples of the border region and the nomadic or seminomadic people beyond, who are forced inland to feed their herds. Well-meant Western proposals to identify "villains" in such cases and impose military reprisals are usually futile. The Rwanda genocide was the result of the hypocrisies of colonialism and of decolonization and "democratization." It was both ethnic in nature and a "class" war between the historically oppressed Hutu and their historic rulers, the Tutsi. The ironic outcome is that the ultimate consequence of the genocidal attack by the democratically empowered Hutu majority upon the Tutsi minority has been to restore Tutsi power in Rwanda. Humanitarian intervention itself often creates problems, as nongovernmental groups now readily acknowledge. UN and NGO action to feed and support refugees and casualties can, for example, reward an aggressor by taking his victims off his hands.

At the time of the U.S. invasion of Iraq, when "humanitarian intervention" continued to be a subject of controversy and political manipulation, the Canadian intellectual and now Liberal Party leader Michael Ignatieff wrote that the United States was the "last hope for democracy and stability" in failed states. Since the Iraq invasion and what has followed, this is no longer a widely held view. Direct American intervention polarizes and politicizes, given not only the widespread present unpopularity of the United States in the non-Western world, but also the frequent incompetence and destructiveness of these interventions.

MY ARGUMENT FROM the beginning of this essay has been that the United States is reenacting in war and politics a classic progression in humanity's collective as well as individual destiny in which the successive stages have consisted in the acquisition of great power—the increasing abuses of power that characterized the Cold War, the Vietnam War, and the eight years of the Bush administration, and thus far of its aftermath, with a subordination of ethical values to an ideology of national triumphalism. A conception of American Manifest Destiny as of universal relevance and validity has been held to justify the arbitrary use of power to impose the national will.

This sequence of events is not the result of any law of history, although humans experience its recurrence. It is recognized in literature, philosophy, and history as a characteristic pattern of human action. What is its culmination? How does it normally end? Aristotle, and the philosophers and artists of his time and before, found "pity and terror" in the artistic representation of such events and a moral catharsis in witnessing their tragic conclusion, considered ineluctable. Can tragedy and failure be avoided in the American case? George Kennan believed that it could if Americans looked within themselves. The nation might eventually discover that it is unable "to find in our relations with other countries or other parts of the world relief from the painful domestic confrontation with ourselves." He wrote in 1993, "We are, for the love of God, only human beings, the descendants of human beings, the bearers, like our ancestors, of all the usual human frailties. Divine hands may occasionally reach down to support us in our struggles, as individuals, with our divided nature; but no divine hand has ever reached down to make us, as a national community, anything more than what we are, or to elevate us in that capacity over the remainder of mankind."[13]

Those were the words of an old man of eighty-nine, whose belief in the American republic remained very much alive. They might find a different validation in the nation's simply becoming so distracted by simultaneous and continuing economic and domestic social crises and loss, and the loss of international economic and financial primacy, that it finds itself forced by uncontrollable forces to abandon military and political fantasy and retreat into a healing isolation.

A second relatively simple possibility is that the nation's attempt by military means to control the evolution of radical and puritanical political forces in Islamic society, as well as the concomitant ills that afflict the modern world elsewhere, might simply exhaust itself in repeated and extensive military frustration. This could take a long time, as the recognition of failure will be resisted, ignored, or distorted in the minds of American leaders and policy thinkers, convinced that power has given them the means to "make new realities" (as the George W. Bush government tried and failed to do), able to overcome the grinding inertia of existing reality. Such would be a further exhibition of pride, one of the components of Hubris, introduction to Nemesis.

Another result of such failures, if accompanied by national humiliation, could produce hatred against those Americans held responsible for the failure, as after America's defeat in Vietnam. One must note that the most intense post-Vietnam hatred was not for those responsible for the war, but for those who had opposed it—and ominously, for those who had fought it: Its veterans to an extent found themselves pariahs, incomprehensibly to themselves. Anger may mount against enemies in the Muslim world, their allies, and their sympathizers, and also against the "so-called allies" who fail to support the United States.

It was not an isolated segment of opinion that expressed the domestic bitterness that followed the Vietnam War. It included leading figures in the Republican Party and inside the army and air force who held the war's opponents responsible for having blocked the measures of unlimited war

they claimed could still have won in Vietnam (to what purpose, as we now have to ask). This certainly could happen
again, and it may even be likely if the war in Asia lengthens,
as the president warned the Veterans of Foreign Wars in
August 2009 that it would.

The Vietnam War aroused an enduring and corrosive
hatred between certain groups of Americans. This hatred
has reappeared since the 2008 presidential election. The
conflicts that have followed have all seemed too intense for
their articulated causes. Some said this was a return of
racism, suppressed during the presidential campaign. I think
not. It was as if a huge, uncomprehending disappointment
lay across the land, especially among the poor and middle
classes who had most believed in the American Dream and
felt most betrayed by what the United States had become
by 2010. I would think this is why Barack Obama has so
stubbornly sought reconciliation and cooperation in governing the nation. This was to be his greatness. He has yet
to find it. In matters of international policy he has followed
the road laid out by his immediate predecessors, and by the
dominant policy elites and interests that already have failed
the nation.

Imperial failure is more likely to begin in detail than in
drama. The Swiss philosopher Denis de Rougemont has
noted that

> one of the minor prophets of the modern era,
> Joseph de Maistre, wrote under Napoleon, "When
> a too preponderant power terrifies the universe,
> one is irritated to find no means to stop it; one
> abounds in bitter reproaches against the egoism

and immorality of governments, which prevent
them from uniting to confront the common danger. But at bottom these complaints are ill-founded.
A coalition among sovereigns, formed on the principles of a pure and disinterested morality, would
be a miracle. God, who owes no one any miracles,
and who makes no useless ones, employs two simple means to reestablish the equilibrium: sometimes the giant cuts his own throat, sometimes a
greatly inferior power throws in his path an imper-
ceptible obstacle which, no one knows how, subsequently grows and becomes insurmountable; like a
feeble reed, caught in the current of a river, which
in the end produces an accumulation of silt which
changes its course."[14]

The United States may simply find itself with no choice
but to fall back on itself, no doubt embittered by disappointment. That might provide a soft ending to empire. The
hard ending would be palpable defeat in crucial undertak-
ings. These would have to be defeats that cut through the in-
sulation of ignorance, misinformation, and complacency that
has prevailed in the country during the first decade of the
new century and such is perhaps impossible. The external
crisis would have to be deeper, and be more personal in its
effects, than the Vietnam defeat, and that too seems unlikely.
The American army thwarted in Vietnam was the people's
army: hence millions of men and their families were involved. It was the corrupted remnant of those American
people's armies that fought the Revolutionary, Civil (on two
sides), and world wars, in which, in this new Vietnam ver-

sion, the privileged of society, and the cowards, stood aside, finding themselves with "other priorities"—as former vice president Richard Cheney told us—and were able to find the complacent doctor, academic dean, or draft board to make it happen. The new all-volunteer American army is working and lower-middle class, and it increasingly is composed of, and recruited from, poor foreigners, in need of a route to legal immigration.

I suppose there could also be a catastrophic end, in which a maddened American elite would show an ungrateful world why all those nuclear weapons had been saved. That is harder to imagine, almost impossible, but as I have suggested, the personalities and ideologies to constitute an elite of revenge-seekers clearly are latent in modern American political society, having already revealed themselves by their responsibility for American torture sites around the world, our hired assassins, and all the others who have pitilessly killed or been killed in empty causes since 2001. Even to speak of such a possibility is confirmation that the post-Enlightenment crisis of Western civilization is not over.

Today the conviction is all but unanimous that the First World War was purposeless, entered into without objective cause and finished in general ruin. Everyone agrees that the totalitarian-instigated Second World War, and the delirious ambitions of those who caused that war, displayed man at his most bestial. What then should we say about today's worldwide struggle between Americans and "the rest" that does not have behind it even a convincing positive ideological cause—such as Marxism-Leninism, which was plausible and seemingly progressive to many in the circumstances of those times? The struggle is not powered by a claim to national vindication after defeat and seeming betrayal—as in Germany's case after 1918, put together by Hitler with a national project of racial conquest, national expansion, and world domination. America's only rationale is that as the sole superpower it seeme inevitable that it impose its own values as universal.

Thucydides, writing of the war between Athens and Sparta, dismisses, as if beyond comment, the evidence of human bestiality loosed on the weak, the arrogance of leaders, the greed of the profiteers, and the criminal complacence of the demagogue, in order to speak of something more important: political stupidity.

The stupidity is "the belief that military measures and massacres can resolve intricate political-territorial contrarieties of interest; the collective folly that seems to infect civic sensibility, making it tribal and infantile, in moments of victory; the incapacity of statecraft and sheer common sense to halt, to reexamine rationally the mechanism of waste and of mutual crippling, which wars set in motion."[13]

Americans today conduct a colossally militarized but morally nugatory global mission supported by apparent majorities of the political, intellectual, and academic elites of the nation. It has lacked from the very beginning an attainable goal. It cannot succeed. George W. Bush is quoted by Bob Woodward as having said that American strategy was "to create chaos, to create vacuum," in his enemies' countries. This was very unwise. The United States risks becoming such a strategy's ultimate victim.

Acknowledgments

I MUST thank George Gibson and Steve Wasserman for their painstaking contributions to the task of drawing coherence from disorder in drafting this book.

I owe a special note of acknowledgment to my friend Patrick Seale, the well-known British writer and authority on the Middle East, for his critical review of what now is chapter V. Needless to say, he bears no responsibility for what I have made of his criticisms.

The book has grown out of an article published in the *New York Review of Books* on February 15, 2007, "Manifest Destiny: A New Direction for America." In it I set down reflections inspired by nearly sixty years of engagement with international affairs and American foreign relations.

My indebtedness to the thought and work of many others dealing with these matters—particular that of George F. Kennan—will be evident (and conscientiously acknowledged, I believe) in my text.

I must finally acknowledge the crucial moral and philosophical influence of Frank O'Malley at Notre Dame so many years ago.

Notes

An Introductory Note

1. Kenneth Minogue, *Alien Powers: The Pure Theory of Ideology* (London: Weidenfeld and Nicolson, 1985).
2. According to Foreign Policy in Focus, Washington, February 2009.
3. "Manifest Destiny" seems to have entered the national political vocabulary as a newspaper editorialist's phrase, first used in 1845 in connection with the annexation of Texas. Stephen Douglas is so quoted in Edmund Wilson, *Patriotic Gore: Studies in the Literature of the American Civil War* (New York: Deutsch, 1962) xxiii.

I. A Manifest Destiny

1. Peter Gay, *The Enlightenment: The Rise of Modern Paganism* (New York: Random House, 1961).
2. In an address by the then U.S. National Security Advisor in London to the 2003 Annual Conference of the International Institute for Security Studies.
3. One of Hannah Arendt's deepest insights into the totalitarian phenomenon concerned its all but total disregard of practicality in state policy. Christopher Lasch writes that she wished to

call special attention to "the astonishing growth of moral and political nihilism, the emergence of the mentality that 'anything is possible,' with its 'indifference even to elementary considerations of political utility and expediency'"—a mentality that exists among many contemporary American policy makers, for whom "reality" is not a constraint; it is merely what is already past. Their "reality" has yet to be created. Introduction to a special issue on Hannah Arendt, "Politics and the Social Contract," *Salmagundi* 60 (1983).

4. There is "virtually no support" for this idea elsewhere in the democracies as Thomas Carothers noted in "A League of Their Own" (*Foreign Policy* July-August 2008). For an eloquent plea for achieving a "global nation," consisting of "multilateralism far beyond anything the world has achieved to date," see Strobe Talbott, *The Great Experiment: The Story of Ancient Empires, Modern States, and the Quest for a Global Nation* (New York: Simon and Schuster, 2009). As is apparent in the present book, I regard this objective as unachieveable, undesirable, and dangerous, but it has seduced American policy elites since at least the time of Woodrow Wilson.

5. George F. Kennan's eight-thousand-word telegram to his superiors in Washington was composed in February 1946 while Ambassador Averell Harriman was absent from Moscow and Kennan was chargé d'affaires. Its reception in Washington was sensational, and it was rapidly circulated through the highest levels of government, becoming the founding document of the Containment policy.

In summer 1947—sixteen months later—its substance was printed as "The Sources of Soviet Conduct" in *Foreign Affairs* (July 1947) under the pseudonym "X." While restrained in tone, and confident that his forecast of eventual Communist collapse would be fulfilled, Kennan emphasized the crucial role of power, noting in the "Long Telegram" that while the

Soviet view of the world was a "neurotic" one, and the Soviet leaders "impervious to the logic of reason," the Kremlin was "highly sensitive to the logic of force. For this reason it can easily withdraw—and usually does—when strong resistance is encountered at any point."

Kennan's initial views on the postwar Soviet Union were set forth both in the "X" article and in the essay "America and the Russian Future," published in *Foreign Affairs* in April 1951. The two were published that year, together with his Walgreen Foundation Lectures at the University of Chicago on American foreign relations, in the volume *American Diplomacy 1900–1950*. His later views appeared in his many books, and notably in *Memoirs: 1925–1950*, published in 1967, *Memoirs: 1950–1963* (1972), a "personal and political philosophy" published in 1993 as *Around the Cragged Hill*, and a final personal volume in 1996, *At a Century's Ending: Reflections 1982–1995*.

The distinguished historian John Lukacs has published his fifty-year correspondence with Kennan concerning the early Cold War in *George F. Kennan and the Origins of Containment 1944–46: The Kennan–Lukacs Correspondence* (1996) as well as a wise and moving appreciation, *George Kennan: A Study of Character* (2007).

6. Simon Serfaty (of the Center for Strategic and International Studies in Washington), "The Pressures for a New Euro-Atlantic Security Strategy," *Europe's World* (Brussels, Summer 2008).

II. The Enlightenment Invention of Secular Utopia

1. The commonly accepted account; however, the argument is made that the Greek legacy was preserved in monastery libraries and known by scholars in the Middle Ages, particularly in southern Italy and Sicily among the Greek Christian

diaspora, and in such Western centers of scriptural and philo-sophical translation as Mont Saint-Michel in France. (See Syl-vain Gouguenheim, *Aristote au Mont Saint-Michel: Les racines grecques de l'Europe chrétienne* (Paris: Seuil, 2008). Aquinas's theological and philosophical work in the thirteenth century rested on Aristotelian foundations.

2. The doctrinal differences were expressed in arbitrary but sig-nificant formulations, such as whether the Holy Spirit "pro-ceeded" from the Son as well as the Father, as the Latin Church held, or simply from the Father, as asserted by the First Ecu-menical Council of Constantinople in 381. This was a matter of great significance to the Eastern Christians, who at the time were defending the divinity of the Holy Spirit against a chal-lenge by Macedonian Christians.

3. John Gray, *Black Mass: Apocalyptic Religion and the Death of Utopia* (New York and London: Farrar, Strauss and Giroux, 2007), 34. The responsibility of religion for modern violence (and much else that blights the world) has been argued in sev-eral recent books (and even on red double-decker London Transport buses), recommending what is called the new athe-ism (Richard Dawkins, *The God Delusion*, and Christopher Hitchens, *God Is Not Great*, for example). Their authors are no-table for their invincible theological and historical ignorance in extrapolating the reality of two thousand years of Christian re-ligion from popular modern superstitions associated with it, as commented upon by secular as well as religious reviewers. Speaking for the defense, the British critic Terry Eagleton wrote that Dawkins "falsely considers that Christianity offers a rival view of the universe to science. Hitchens makes the same crass error . . . Christianity was never meant to be an ex-planation of anything . . . It's rather like saying that thanks to the electric toaster we can forget about Chekhov." He accuses the two "of superstition in their belief in the march of

progress; their commitment to individual freedom . . . is an article of faith that has no grounding in science" (*Commonweal* March 27, 2009).

4. Norman Cohn, *The Pursuit of the Millennium* (Oxford: Oxford University Press, 1957). The Anabaptists were a sixteenth-century sect that rejected the efficacy of infant baptism and re-baptised its adherents as adults, by immersion. It soon divided into several currents. The Anabaptists were distant forerunners of the mainstream Baptist movement of the seventeenth century in Britain, which preached the total liberty of the individual to interpret the sole source of religious truth, the Bible. The Flagellants were adepts of violent and public physical penances and were a recurrent marginal Christian phenomenon, beginning in Italy and Germany in the thirteenth and fourteenth centuries. Among Muslims, self-flagellation is a practice during the annual Shiite penitential observation of the failure to save from death Husayn, son of the sect's founder, Ali, supposedly the rightful successor to Muhammad.

5. Guglielmo Ferrero, *The Gamble: Bonaparte in Italy, 1796–1797*. Trans. Bertha Pritchard and Lily C. Freeman. (New York: Walker & Company, 1961) 297–299.

6. Luigi Barzini, an author and famous journalist who knew Mussolini, wrote: "He was perhaps the best popular journalist of his day in Italy, addressing himself not to the sober cultured minority but to the practically illiterate masses . . . Those very qualities that made him an excellent rabble-rousing editor made him a disastrous statesman: his intuitive and superficial intelligence; his capacity to oversimplify and dramatize; a day-to-day interest only in the most striking events; a strictly partisan point of view; the disregard for truth, accuracy, objectivity and consistency when they interfered with his aims; . . . an instinctive ability . . . to know what people wanted to be told . . . [Of course he] used deceit as a tool to govern with . . . All

great statesmen have had recourse to occasional distortions, misinterpretations and outright lies. Mussolini merely lied more than all other past statesmen, a little more than some of his contemporary competitors, less than Hitler anyway . . . He, too, believed his own slogans. He, too, was amazed by the fake statistics, thrilled by empty boasts, stirred to tears by his own oratory. He, too, confused appearances for reality . . . It is well known that Hitler's favorable opinion of his partner, of Italian military preparations, and the [Italian] people's devotion to the régime and to the Axis, made him commit fatal miscalculations, one of which probably cost him the war. He believed, in the end, that he lost the Russian campaign because he had started four weeks too late; he was four weeks late because he wasted time to rescue the Italians bogged down in Albania, in their ill-prepared attack on Greece. If this were true, Mussolini could be considered the greatest negative military genius the world has ever seen, who defeated two great nations single-handed, his own and Germany . . . Thirteen years before his death he had told [the writer] Emil Ludwig: 'Everybody dies the death that corresponds to his character.' He had deluded the people, that was his crime. But his fatal error was that he had not known that the people were also deluding him. They led him to the catastrophe which was the only way they knew to get rid of him." Barzini in The Italians (New York: Atheneum, 1964).

7. Arthur Koestler, *Arrow in the Blue: An Autobiography* (New York: Macmillan, 1961). In addition to *Darkness at Noon*, his celebrated, politically plausible and psychologically penetrating novel about the Stalinist show trials. (As it turned out, it was mistaken in its attribution of political motivation to its main character's false show-trial confession, supposedly made to protect the Party. Such confessions usually were extracted by torture or threats to the victim's family.) Koestler in 1951

published *The Age of Longing*, a novel set in postwar Paris that includes an equally plausible portrait of a convinced prewar Nazi. The Nazi officer enthusiastically describes Europe's future unification and transformation by Nazi Germany (which ironically, in scope and ambition, was not unlike that of the present-day democratic European Union, enabled and inspired by Nazism's destruction of the Europe of 1940).

III. The Sources of America's Moral and Political Isolation from Europe

1. "The European Vision of America" was organized by the Cleveland Museum of Art with the collaboration of the National Gallery of Art, Washington, D.C., and the Réunion des musées nationaux, Paris. It was shown at the National Gallery of Art from December 7, 1975, to February 15, 1976; at the Cleveland Museum of Art, from May 6 to August 8, 1976; and as "L'Amerique vue par l'Europe," at the Galeries nationales du Grand-Palais in Paris, from September 17, 1976, to January 3, 1977.

2. Perry Miller, *The Life of the Mind in America: From the Revolution to the Civil War* (New York: Harvest, 1965) 4–5. The passage from Robert Baird is quoted by Miller from Baird's *Religion in America* (1844).

3. Mark A. Noll, *American Evangelical Christianity: An Introduction* (Hoboken, NJ: Wiley-Blackwell, 2001), quoted in a review by Ralph C. Wood, *First Things* (October 2001). With respect to the Franklin Constitutional Convention motion that failed, one can remark that Hannah Arendt has contrasted the "clear signs of divine origin" in the Declaration of Independence's invocation of "the Laws of Nature and of Nature's God" with the desacralization of the political she saw as characteristic of

modernity (David Armitage, "Birthday of Principle," *Times Literary Supplement* July 6, 2007).

4. Alfred Kazin, *An American Procession* (New York: Alfred A. Knopf, 1984).

5. The *Richmond Dispatch,* with the largest circulation of any newspaper in the Confederacy, commented in early 1863 on "the incongruous and discordant elements out of which the framers of the Constitution sought to create a homogeneous people. The great wonder is not that the two sections have fallen asunder at last, but that they held together so long. The dissimilarity between the moral constitutions, habits of thought, breeding and manners of the Cavalier and Round-head must run in the blood for generations, and defy all the glue and cement of political unions" (February 27 and March 23). The historian James M. McPherson also quotes the Confederate soldier's letter urging his wife in 1862 to teach their children "a bitter and unrelenting hatred of the Yankee race . . . so vile and cursed race" (letter by Captain Elijah P. Petty). Both in McPherson, review of works of the late George M. Frederickson in the *New York Review of Books* (December 4, 2008).

6. Bryan as a populist progressive advocated the income tax, woman's suffrage, free coinage of silver, and anti-imperialism, as well as Prohibition, but in 1925 he volunteered to testify in the celebrated Scopes "monkey trial" in Tennessee, where a young teacher, John Thomas Scopes, was charged with teaching evolution in violation of a just-passed state law. Under the baiting questioning of Scopes's attorney, Clarence Darrow, Bryan, as a witness for the prosecution, defended the literal truth of the book of Genesis's account of creation and affirmed his personal belief that this event had taken place in 4004 B.C., that the Flood occurred around 2348 B.C., and that Jonah had indeed been swallowed by "a big fish." The judge

took pity, stopped the questioning, and struck it from the record. He found Scopes guilty, and fined him $100. The Tennessee Supreme Court later sustained the law but freed Scopes on a technicality, preventing a further appeal. Bryan died five days after the trial. Needless to say this settled nothing; during the presidential primary campaign in 2008 the genial ex-governor of Arkansas and one-time Baptist preacher Mike Huckabee, who won the Republican caucus nomination in the Iowa primary, was asked about evolution. He replied, "If people want to believe they're descended from a primate, they can go right ahead." (He did not disclose the species of his own parents.)

7. Review of Richard Kyle, *Evangelicalism: An Americanized Christianity* (New York and London: Transaction, 2006), in the *Times Literary Supplement* (June 8, 2007).

IV. From American Isolationism to Utopian Interventionism

1. See R. S. Baker, *Woodrow Wilson and the World Settlement*, vol. 1 (Garden City, NY: Doubleday, Page & Co., 1922), 18.

2. Walter Millis, *The Road to War: 1914–1917*, (New York: Houghton Mifflin, 1935).

3. George F. Kennan, "America and the Orient," *American Diplomacy 1900–1950*, (Chicago: University of Chicago Press, 1951), 49.

4. See entry on R. A. Taft in the *Columbia Encyclopedia*, fifth ed. (New York, 1975).

5. Kennan, "The Sources of Soviet Conduct." What later was said in criticism of Kennan and Containment by armchair warriors—"a policy of sitting atop a hill and leading by example, in practice of a policy of cowardice and dishonor," according

to William Kristol and Robert Kagan (*Foreign Affairs*, July–
August 1996)—is actually a criticism of the Republican John
Foster Dulles, who was secretary of state from 1953 to 1959, the
time about which Kristol and Kagan wrote. Kennan was a major influence in the post–Second World War reorganization of
American clandestine intelligence services and was regarded
as the "father" of the Free Europe Committee's radio, press,
and organizational political warfare operations, and of other
CIA initiatives to counter the widespread and influential Comintern propaganda of the period (which was very effective, especially in liberated Western Europe; the present writer was
for a time in the mid-1950s an executive at the committee).

Kennan left the State Department by 1953, after Moscow
had rejected his appointment as U.S. ambassador (he knew
too much!). His influence was replaced by that of another
diplomat, Paul Nitze, who, according to a recent book by
Nicholas Thompson, Nitze's grandson, was author of the policy document (NSC 68) and chiefly responsible for the huge
buildup of American military power and shift of emphasis to
military force replacing Kennan's political Containment policies, (*The Hawk and the Dove: Paul Nitze, George Kennan, and the
History of the Cold War*, New York: Henry Holt and Co.,
2009). When the Berlin Wall fell, Kennan said, "I believe it
would have happened earlier, if we had not militarized the rivalry."

6. Edmund Stillman and William Pfaff, *The New Politics: America
and the End of the Postwar World* (New York and London:
Coward-McCann and Victor Bollancz, 1961). Among other
critics of the established policy of the period were the Christian realist Reinhold Niebuhr (whom Kennan called "the father of us all"), Louis Halle, Ronald Steel (whose important
books *The End of Alliance* and *Pax Americana* appeared in 1964
and 1966, respectively), and to a qualified extent, as the Viet-

nam War developed, Walter Lippmann, the columnist. The most important recent critics of interventionism include Chalmers Johnson; John Newhouse; Anatol Lieven (*America Right or Wrong: An Anatomy of American Nationalism*, New York: Oxford University Press, 2004); Lieven and John Hulsman (*Ethical Realism*, New York: Pantheon, 2006); and Andrew Bacevich (*The Limits of Power: The End of American Exceptionalism*, New York: Metropolitan Books, 2008, and *The New American Militarism: How Americans Are Seduced by War*, New York: Oxford University Press, 2005).

7. Washington policy ignored the so-called Sino-Soviet split that had developed rapidly after Stalin's death in 1953 and that was deepened by the "Secret Speech" denouncing Stalin, made by First Secretary Nikita Khrushchev at the Community Party's Twentieth Congress in 1956. The divergence between the Maoist government and post-Stalinist Russia rested fundamentally on different national as well as party interests, but official Washington at this period was so mesmerized by Communist ideology as to refuse the notion that national interest could prevail over ideology. This blindness caused the American failure to recognize that the Communist Viet Minh and Viet Cong in Indochina were fundamentally motivated by nationalism, with Communism being the vehicle for mobilizing and disciplining the national resistance. This conceptual error was responsible for the prolonged U.S. involvement in that war, with its deeply tragic consequences for Vietnam, Laos, and Cambodia as well as for Americans.

8. John Gray in a review in the *New York Review of Books* (October 9, 2008) of Leszek Kolakowski, *Why Is There Something Rather Than Nothing?: 23 Questions from Great Philosophers* (New York: Basic Books, 2008).

9. Bush policy was greatly influenced by the opportune publication of a book by the former Soviet dissident and Israeli political

figure Natan Sharansky, arguing that international stability is possible only when democracy prevails. (Sharansky with Ron Dermer, *The Case for Democracy: The Power of Freedom to Overcome Tyranny and Terror*, New York: Public Affairs, 2004.) This is a pleasing thought but has no evidence to sustain it. The United States, for example, is a democracy, and yet, in part under the influence of this proposition, is the greatest national source of instability in the contemporary world because of its efforts to impose stability on others who do not want it in its American form. The Sharansky book came to the attention of the White House at a convenient moment, when the failure to find weapons of mass destruction in Iraq was having an electoral impact.

In a talk given at the Woodrow Wilson Scholars' Center following the Soviet collapse, Alan Greenspan said: "The dismantling of the central planning function in an economy does not, as some had supposed, automatically establish [market capitalism]. After 1989 we discovered that much of what we took for granted in our free market system and assumed to be human nature was not nature at all but culture." Mr. Greenspan had actually discovered not the force of culture but of sin— original sin, which the theologian Reinhold Niebuhr has described as "the one empirically verifiable Christian tenet."

10. The India-Pakistan case is an exception since the perceived threat is strictly bilateral, and the concerned countries have simply replicated for themselves, at great expense, the "balance of terror" that existed between the United States and the Soviet Union during the Cold War.

The danger of terrorist-held nuclear weapons exists, if barely. It would require the complicity of a nuclear state, and the political plausibility of any government allowing terrorists to control such weapons seems next to nil, while the technical and logistical complexity of such an operation would be great. In any case there is little to be done about the possibility that is not already being done. In nuclear military matters one would do well to consult the writings of my former colleague, the late Herman Kahn, whose exhaustive and deliberately provocative analyses are the reference for serious consideration of the subject. However, most discussion of "rogue-state" nuclear weapons is simple scare-mongering, meant to promote fear of and hostility toward countries that the nation issuing such propaganda wishes to undermine for entirely different reasons. Iraq and Iran provide obvious examples of such manipulation.

V. America's Elected Enemy

1.   Samuel P. Huntington, *The Clash of Civilizations and the Remaking of World Order* (New York: Touchstone, 1996).
2.   David Levering Lewis, "Islam and the Making of the First Europe, A Counter-Narrative," *Berlin Journal* (Spring 2008). Adapted from Lewis, *God's Crucible: Islam and the Making of Europe, 570 to 1215* (New York: W.W. Norton & Co., 2008).
3.   Noah Feldman, *The Fall and Rise of the Islamic State* (Princeton, N.J.: Princeton University Press, 2008). Feldman is a jurist and historian, Bemis Professor of International Law at Harvard.
4.   Malise Ruthven, "The Rise of the Muslim Terrorists," *New York Review of Books* (May 29, 2008).
5.   Feldman, *The Fall and Rise of the Islamic State.*
6.   Chen Tu-hsiu, accepted leader of the literary renaissance associated with the National Peking University (established 1898). Quoted in K. Madhu Panikkar, *Asia and Western Dominance: A Survey of the Vasco da Gama Epoch of Asian History, 1498–1945* (London: George, Allen & Unwin, 1953).

7. See Stanley Karnow, *Vietnam: A History* (New York: Viking, 1983).

8. Wendy Kristianasen, "Who Is a Salafist?" *Le Monde diplomatique* (English Edition), Paris, February 3, 2008. See also Samuel Helfont, "The Sunni Divide: Understanding Politics and Terrorism in the Arab Middle East," Foreign Policy Research Institute, November 2009.

9. Malise Ruthven, "The Rise of the Muslim Terrorist."

10. Jean-Pierre Filiu, "Hizb ut-Tahrir and the Fantasy of the Caliphate," *Le Monde diplomatique* (English edition), Paris, June 2008.

11. Henry Kissinger, op-ed, *International Herald Tribune* (April 7, 2008).

12. Condoleezza Rice, address to the Annual Convention of the International Institute for Strategic Studies, London, 2003.

13. McCain quoted in David Whitford, "The Evolution of John McCain," *Fortune*, June 28, 2008.

14. Philip Bobbitt, *Terror and Consent: The Wars for the Twenty-first Century* (New York and London: Knopf, 2008).

15. Bruce Riedel, "Armageddon in Islamabad," *National Interest*, Washington, D.C., July–August 2009.

16. Pankaj Mishra, *The Guardian*, London, August 7, 2009.

17. Mark Lilla, *The Stillborn God: Religion, Politics, and the Modern West* (New York: Random House, 2007).

VI. How It Ends

1. Mr. Brzezinski himself claimed responsibility for the mujahideen uprising against the Soviet occupation of Afghanistan in an interview with the Paris weekly *Le Nouvel Observateur* (January 15–21, 1998). "The reality, secretly guarded until now, [is that] it was July 3, 1979, that President Carter signed

the first directive for secret aid to the opponents of the pro-Soviet regime in Kabul. And that very day, I wrote a note to the president in which I explained to him that in my opinion this aid was going to induce a Soviet military intervention . . . We didn't push the Russians to intervene, but we knowingly increased the probability that they would" as translated by the present writer, *New York Review of Books*, April 8, 2004.

2. Joseph Schumpeter, *Imperialism and Social Classes* (New York: A.M. Kelly, 1951). "Fifty years ago . . ." from Stillman and Pfaff, *The New Politics*.

3. Andrew Bacevich, in his introduction to Bacevich, ed., *The Long War: A New History of U.S. National Security Policy Since World War II* (New York: Columbia University Press, 2007), xii.

4. My remarks about the American army are not meant to denigrate the institution but to comment upon how it has been used. I myself had a long and positive association with the U.S. Army, donning its uniform at the age of fourteen, in Junior ROTC in a Southern army town, and taking the uniform off for the last time at the age of twenty-eight, leaving the active reserve.

5. John Lewis Gaddis, *Surprise, Security, and the American Experience* (Cambridge Mass.: Harvard University Press, 2004).

6. Alfred Vagts, *A History of Militarism, Civilian and Military*, rev. ed. (New York: Meridian Books, 1959) 13–15. William Lind quoted by Chalmers Johnson in an interview published on the Web site www.Tomdispatch, March 2, 2009.

7. Robert G. Kaiser, *So Damned Much Money: The Triumph of Lobbying and the Corrosion of American Government* (New York: Random House, 2009). See also John R. MacArthur, *You Can't Be President: The Outrageous Barriers to Democracy in America* (Brooklyn, New York: Melville House Publishing, 2008). Kaiser is the associate editor of the *Washington Post* and MacArthur is the publisher of *Harper's* magazine.

8. John Kenneth Galbraith, *Name-Dropping* (Boston: Houghton Mifflin Harcourt, 1999).

9. Claes G. Ryn, *America the Virtuous: The Crisis of Democracy and the Quest for Empire* (New Brunswick and London: Transaction Publishers, 2003). For a splendid account of the neoconservatives' origins and the influence of Leo Strauss, see Anne Norton, *Leo Strauss and the Politics of American Empire* (New Haven, Conn., and London: Yale University Press, 2004).

10. Christopher Caldwell, "The Politics of Self-Abasement," *Financial Times,* June 5, 2009.

11. George F. Kennan, *Around the Cragged Hill: A Personal and Political Philosophy* (New York and London: W.W. Norton and Company, Inc., 1993), chapter 9, passim.

12. Former Israeli prime minister Ehud Olmert said on September 29, 2008, what "everybody" had already known but no Israeli leader in power had had the courage to say: "That Israel must withdraw from nearly all of the West Bank and East Jerusalem to attain peace with the Palestinians and that any occupied land that it held on to would have to be exchanged for the same quantity of Israeli territory." Interview in the newspaper *Yediot Aharonot,* as reported in the *International Herald Tribune* on September 30, 2008. Unfortunately, Olmert on September 29, 2008, was caretaker prime minister and was incapable of acting on his words.

13. Kennan, *Around the Cragged Hill.*

14. *The Devil's Share: An Essay on the Diabolic in Modern Society* (Washington, D.C.: Bollingen Series of the Old Dominion Foundation,1994), 199–200. Copyright assigned to Bollingen Foundation, Inc., New York, NY. Meridian edition first published March 1956.

15. See George Steiner, review of Donald Kagan, *The Peloponnesian War,* in the *New Yorker,* March 11, 1991.

Index

lessons of, 105
post-Vietnam hatreds, 186–187
vigilantes, 59–60
violence, international. *See* war and
violence, international
violence, in U.S., 57–60

Wahhabism, 128, 129, 137–138
war and violence, international.
See also specific wars and conflicts
within Christianity, 24–25,
31–32
in Cold War, xii–xiii
democracy and ideology of peace,
88
democratic expansionism and,
13–14
Enlightenment and rise of modern violence, 6, 10
foreign intrusion and occupation,
resistance to, 122–127
imperialism and, 156–157
limited and instrumental, ended
by French Revolution, 32–33
noninterventionist policy alternative, 177–184
redefined "on our terms"
(Bush), 105
religion blamed for, 196n3
religious warfare, purpose of,
26–27
secular vs. religious, 27
shift from defense to fantasies of
omnipotence, 172
war on terror. *See also* Afghan-
Pakistan war; Iraq war;
terrorism

American interests and goals,
165–170
"clash of civilizations" theory,
104–110
new caliphate notion and,
134–136
as parody of Cold War, 82–83
as product of ignorance and
political confusion, 84
theory of inborn Islamic violence, 123
Trotskyism and, 37n
unexplained, 109–110
Washington, George, 44, 46, 48
Waziristan, 138
Wedgwood, C. V., 32
West, U.S., 58–59, 69
Western civilization, size of,
106
Westphalian system, 7, 7n, 136
Wharton, Edith, 55
Wilson, Woodrow, 34, 67–68,
70–74, 71n, 168
Winthrop, John, 23n, 44
Wood, Ralph C., 51
world order, new, 10
World Trade Center attack (1993),
139
World War I, 34, 68, 70–74
World War II, 74–75

Yemen, 143
Young Turk movement, 119,
121
Yugoslav wars, 38, 182–183

Zakaria, Rafia, 147

A Note on the Author

WILLIAM PFAFF was born in Iowa, grew up in Georgia, and served in infantry and Special Forces units of the U.S. Army during and after the Korean War. He received a B.A. degree in the Philosophy of Literature and in Political Studies from the University of Note Dame.

He has been an editor of *Commonweal* magazine, an executive of the political warfare organization the Free Europe Committee, one of the earliest members of the Hudson Institute, and subsequently deputy director of its European affiliate in Paris, Hudson Research Europe.

From 1971 to 1992 he contributed more than seventy "Reflections" on political matters to William Shawn's *New Yorker*. He is also a longtime contributor to the *New York Review of Books*. He wrote a featured and syndicated editorial page column for the *International Herald Tribune* from 1978 until 2003, when his columns concerning the invasion of Iraq led to a break with the newspaper's new owners, the New York Times Company, who ruled that the *Herald Tribune* could no longer publish his articles on matters of American foreign policy and foreign relations.

In 2006 the American Academy of Diplomacy in

Washington gave him its Arthur Ross Award for Distinguished Analysis of Foreign Affairs, saying, "Few can rival his impact on thinking about the deepest dilemmas of foreign policy and of prime movers in human society. We are inspired by his moral vision of the proper uses of power and limits on its abuse."

The Irony of Manifest Destiny is his ninth book. His *Barbarian Sentiments* was a finalist for the 1989 National Book Award, and in French translation won the City of Geneva's annual Prix du Jean-Jacques Rousseau.

He is married to the former Carolyn Cleary, a writer and gardener. They have two children and five grandchildren.